Seeing Students Learn Science

Integrating Assessment and Instruction in the Classroom

Alexandra Beatty and Heidi Schweingruber

Based on the National Research Council Report
Developing Assessments for the Next Generation Science Standards

Board on Science Education

Board on Testing and Assessment

Division of Behavioral and Social Sciences and Education

The National Academies of
SCIENCES · ENGINEERING · MEDICINE

THE NATIONAL ACADEMIES PRESS
Washington, DC
www.nap.edu

THE NATIONAL ACADEMIES PRESS   500 Fifth Street, NW   Washington, DC 20001

This activity was supported by Grant No. B9053 from the Carnegie Corporation of New York. Any opinions, findings, conclusions, or recommendations expressed in this publication do not necessarily reflect the views of any organization or agency that provided support for the project.

Library of Congress Cataloging-in-Publication Data

Names: Beatty, Alexandra S., author. | Schweingruber, Heidi A., author.
Title: Seeing students learn science : integrating assessment and instruction
  in the classroom / Alexandra Beatty and Heidi Schweingruber
Description: Washington, DC : National Academies Press, [2016] | "Based on
  the National Research Council Report Developing Assessments for the Next
  Generation Science Standards Board on Science Education Board on Testing
  and Assessment Division of Behavioral and Social Sciences and Education."
  | "A Report of The National Academies of Sciences, Engineering, and
  Medicine." | Includes bibliographical references and index.
Identifiers: LCCN 2016056188 | ISBN 9780309444323 (pbk.) | ISBN 9780309444330
  (pdf)
Subjects: LCSH: Science—Study and teaching (Elementary)—United States. |
  Science—Study and teaching (Secondary)—United States. | Science—Study
  and teaching—United States—Evaluation.
Classification: LCC LB1585.3 .B39 2017 | DDC 372.35/044—dc23
LC record available at https://lccn.loc.gov/2016056188

Digital Object Identifier: 10.17226/23548

Additional copies of this publication are available for sale from the National Academies Press, 500 Fifth Street, NW, Keck 360, Washington, DC 20001; (800) 624-6242 or (202) 334-3313; http://www.nap.edu.

Suggested citation: National Academies of Sciences, Engineering, and Medicine. 2017. *Seeing Students Learn Science: Integrating Assessment and Instruction in the Classroom*. Washington, DC: The National Academies Press. doi: 10.17226/23548.

The National Academies of
SCIENCES · ENGINEERING · MEDICINE

The **National Academy of Sciences** was established in 1863 by an Act of Congress, signed by President Lincoln, as a private, nongovernmental institution to advise the nation on issues related to science and technology. Members are elected by their peers for outstanding contributions to research. Dr. Marcia McNutt is president.

The **National Academy of Engineering** was established in 1964 under the charter of the National Academy of Sciences to bring the practices of engineering to advising the nation. Members are elected by their peers for extraordinary contributions to engineering. Dr. C. D. Mote, Jr., is president.

The **National Academy of Medicine** (formerly the Institute of Medicine) was established in 1970 under the charter of the National Academy of Sciences to advise the nation on medical and health issues. Members are elected by their peers for distinguished contributions to medicine and health. Dr. Victor J. Dzau is president.

The three Academies work together as the **National Academies of Sciences, Engineering, and Medicine** to provide independent, objective analysis and advice to the nation and conduct other activities to solve complex problems and inform public policy decisions. The National Academies also encourage education and research, recognize outstanding contributions to knowledge, and increase public understanding in matters of science, engineering, and medicine.

Learn more about the National Academies of Sciences, Engineering, and Medicine at **www.national-academies.org**.

Preface

Science educators in the United States are adapting to a new vision of how students learn science. Children are natural explorers, and their observations and intuitions about the world around them are the foundation for science learning. Unfortunately, the way science has been taught in the United States has not always taken advantage of those attributes. Some students who successfully complete their K–12 science classes have not really had the chance to "do" science for themselves in ways that harness their natural curiosity and understanding of the world around them.

A 2012 report, *A Framework for K–12 Science Education*, described a way to teach science (see Box P-1). Many educators were already familiar with the ideas in this framework, but it offered specific guidance about what the results of decades of research mean for classroom practice. Many districts and states are using the ideas in that report to make changes that will engage students in thinking and solving problems the way scientists and engineers do and will help them better see how science is relevant to their lives. This approach capitalizes on the natural curiosity all students have about the world around them and helps educators provide varied learning experiences that offer entry points for students from diverse backgrounds.

The 2012 framework served as the blueprint for the development of the Next Generation Science Standards (NGSS). Many states, schools, and districts are changing curriculum, instruction, and professional development to align with these standards or others that are based on the framework. Some states that have not adopted the NGSS are using the 2012 framework to adapt their own standards to these ideas about how students learn science.

No matter how states are adapting, assessments are also changing, and in exciting ways. Existing assessments—whatever their purpose—cannot be used to measure the full range of activities and interactions that are happening in science classrooms that have adapted to these ideas because they were not designed to do so. Many teachers are using excellent assessment tools, but these will need to be adapted to measure this different kind of learning. New assessment methods will also support teachers in adapting their instruction to this vision. The change needed is not only a revision in strategies for all forms of science assessment, but also a different way of thinking about the progress of students' science proficiency. This new thinking is as important for the work that science teachers do in the classroom every day as it is for large-scale accountability assessments.

Assessments are simply ways to collect evidence about what students have learned, and you, as a professional educator, already use them every day in your classroom. This book was written to help you improve your understanding of how your students are learning. New assessment strategies can enrich your instruction while you are adapting it, whether or not your state and district are adopting the NGSS or other new standards.

Adapting your instruction and approach to assessment is likely to be a gradual process. The ideas in this book can help you work with your colleagues to start incorporating new assessment thinking into your instructional practice right now. The material in this book is based on a report from the National Research Council, *Developing Assessments for the Next Generation Science Standards*. The committee of researchers and educators who wrote that report analyzed the research in detail and reviewed the innovative work of many researchers and practitioners who have developed new kinds of assessments. The report provided detailed analysis and recommendations.

This book describes the ideas from that report that classroom teachers can use right now, and that principals, district administrators, and pre- and in-service providers can use to support teachers. It's filled with examples of innovative assessment formats, ways to embed assessments in engaging classroom activities, and ideas for interpreting and using novel kinds of assessment information. It provides ideas and questions educators can use to reflect on what they can adapt right away and what they can work toward more gradually.

The book is organized around some key questions educators have about the new types of assessments:

What's really different? Chapter 1 gives a quick overview of how ideas about science learning and instruction have changed and why different kinds of assessments are needed.

What does this kind of assessment look like? In Chapter 2 we look at a few examples to see how these ideas and principles work in practice.

What can I learn from my students' work? In Chapter 3 we look more deeply at the sorts of information you can get from different types of assessments—how they give you evidence of your students' thinking.

How can I build new kinds of assessments into the flow of my instruction? Chapter 4 describes ways to adapt assessments you already use and to design different ones that will support the changes you are making in your instruction.

How can I work with others in my school, district, and state? In Chapter 5 we focus on how your efforts can interact with what is happening outside your classroom. We look at assessment systems, ways of reporting assessment results, and assessment for monitoring purposes.

Contents

1

What's Really Different?

A group of second-grade students were engaged in an animated discussion. Their teacher had brought in some colorful ears of corn she wanted to use to decorate their classroom for Thanksgiving.[1] But, she explained, she had left the corn outside and it had gotten wet in the rain. She wondered what might happen to it, and whether she could still use it to decorate the classroom. As they discussed the problem, the students asked questions and made assertions.

Some students thought the corn was ruined and might "rot and get stinky." Others thought it would "get darker because it's going to die" or "turn black because water makes stains." One suggested that "it might grow because it has water," but another doubted it would grow and wondered, "Is it fake corn?" A student asked whether "people do something differently or grow it differently [so that] real corn could became all different colors?" The class decided they should "observe it every day" to see "did the colors change" and "draw sci-agrams [science diagrams] to show what's happening" and then "draw models at every stage so we can teach people what happened." Figure 1-1 shows how the teacher captured the students' discussion and what they decided to do to solve their problem.

Over the next few days, the students noticed something happening to the corn (see Figures 1-2 and 1-3) and became even more excited. They noticed that some green things were growing out of the corn and thought these looked like leaves. They also observed that brown things were growing out of the bottom of the corn, toward the water, and some students thought these must be roots.

---

[1]This description is a summary of classroom experiences in the second-grade classrooms of Lori Farkash, Nancy Jo Michael, and Ruth Purdie-Dyer, who worked with Brian Reiser and Michael Novak to develop a three-dimensional storyline intended to involve their students in science practices to get at key elements of the disciplinary core ideas about plant growth. Their storyline, with examples of student work, can be downloaded at http://www.nextgenstorylines.org/why-is-our-corn-changing [April 2016].

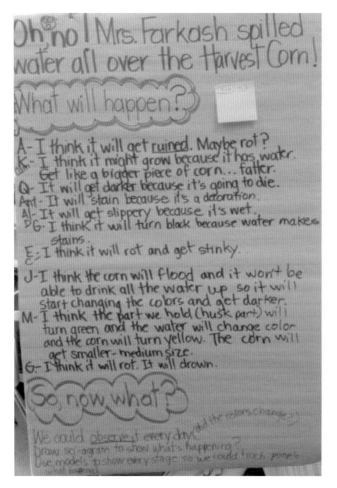

FIGURE 1-1 Documentation of corn discussion.

SOURCE: Farkash et al. (2016). Reprinted with permission.

Each day the students rushed to see what was happening with the corn, and their teacher encouraged them to try to explain what they were seeing. One day a new finding led to a vigorous debate. The students had agreed that somehow the corn was "growing" and must in some way be "alive." But they disagreed about what part of the corn was actually growing. Some students thought that each leaf was coming from an individual piece of corn (which the class learned are called "kernels"). Other students, however, responded that this meant that each kernel was like a seed, and it didn't make sense for a plant to have so many seeds. Still other students pointed out the kernels falling off the cob, and they reasoned that something inside the corncob was growing and maybe pushing off the kernels as it grew. The class decided they needed to do a "fair test" to figure out where the leaves and roots were growing from.

The teacher encouraged them to brainstorm ways to conduct a fair test that would answer their questions. Students wrote and drew their ideas in their journals and then discussed them as a group. After some discussion the class came up with the idea of separately planting some kernels in one pot and pieces of the corncob in another pot to see which would grow. But then they discovered even more things they were not sure about. Should they plant these in soil? Would light be important? They were pretty sure water was important, given the evidence so far. From talking through these possibilities, they realized they needed even more fair tests. They decided to get some "regular" seeds—ones they knew for certain were seeds—and see what they needed in order to grow. Then they could set up the same conditions with the kernels and the corncob to see which part of the corn is the seed.

FIGURE 1-2 The wet corn after a few days.
SOURCE: Farkash et al. (2016). Reprinted with permission.

FIGURE 1-3 The corn with additional growth.
SOURCE: Farkash et al. (2016). Reprinted with permission.

What these second-grade students were doing may not look radically different from what happens in many lively science classrooms. They were describing experiments that are common in many elementary classrooms: exploring whether plants need soil, water, or light to grow. What is important about this scenario, though, is that the students were engaged in this investigation in an attempt to make sense of something they had observed. They were comparing different growth conditions not because they were told to or were given the opportunity to pick a variable they could manipulate; rather, the students themselves identified the need to resolve a question, and the teacher supported them in designing an experiment that would resolve it.

Figure 1-1 shows part of the record the teacher made of the class discussion in which the students decided how to explore their questions about the corn.

Where does assessment fit into this picture? This teacher is using what the students say and do in this activity as part of an assessment of how well they can actually do science for themselves. The students have identified a question they wanted to answer because they observed something puzzling, and they have figured out a way to tackle it. They used what they know about investigation, argumentation, and explanation. They connected it to what they already know and are learning about the needs of living things. As the students engage in these various practices, the teacher is able to assess how they connect claims to evidence, how they connect their explanation of the new evidence to what they have previously figured out about plants, and how well they can develop a plan for an experiment. In other words, the work the students produce as part of their learning also provides valuable information the teacher can use to assess their learning.

This way of embedding the assessment within the learning tasks reflects new ways to think about what a classroom science assessment can be:

- a tool for you as a teacher to collect information about what and how your students are learning;

- a way to help your students see what they've learned;

- a way to help your class figure out where they are in an investigation; and

- a tool for you to use in deciding on next steps for instruction and identifying the supports individual students need.

In other words, assessment can be an integral part of your teaching practice, rather than an interruption.

This approach to assessment reflects the thinking about science learning and instruction described in *A Framework for K–12 Science Education* (National Research Council, 2012) and new science standards that many states and districts are adopting—in many cases, the Next Generation Science Standards (NGSS).[2] In guiding her students to explore what they observed about the corn, the teacher in the example has actively involved students in the practices of science in the way those two documents describe: the students design experiments, collect data, make inferences from the data, and so on. She is also using these tasks to assess learning that cannot be measured by traditional assessments that rely on multiple-choice and other types of selected-response questions.

This chapter describes what is different about this kind of learning and why it means that different thinking about science assessment is needed. It explores the characteristics that assessments need to have if they are to measure this kind of learning, and how this kind of assessment supports instruction. This chapter also describes some basic principles to guide assessment of how students' learning develops, and it looks at how those principles fit with the existing principles of good testing practice.

---

[2]The Next Generation Science Standards (NGSS) are available online at http://www.nextgenscience.org [March 2016].

A NEW WAY TO THINK ABOUT SCIENCE LEARNING

The purpose of new standards for science education—whether the NGSS or similar ones developed by states—is not just to rearrange the order in which topics are taught across the grades. These standards are based on current understanding of *how* kids learn—and how science teaching can reflect the way scientists and engineers do their work. They are designed so that students will do science themselves, not just learn about how other people have done it or memorize facts. Good teachers have always known that learning doesn't happen in a tidy, straight line, but now research has given us ways to describe science learning more accurately. A key idea from that research is that in order for learning to really "stick," students need continuous opportunities to engage in scientific thinking and practices and to gradually build their understanding of how new knowledge fits with what they already know.[3]

Scientists and engineers have a lot of specialized knowledge and skills. But what makes them experts is not that they have command of a lot of facts or are especially skillful at using technical equipment or performing experiments. These experts have had years of study and experience that give them a broad understanding of how the science ideas and practices they have learned fit together. They have developed the capacity to use their understanding and expertise to form and investigate hypotheses, solve problems, and develop new knowledge.

To be science literate is to be able to see how and why science and engineering really matter, to know how to reason from evidence, and to have a sense of how scientists and engineers do what they do. This understanding of science is not only important for students as they progress in secondary and postsecondary science study. When they are adults, today's students will need to apply their capacity to think scientifically about important global challenges—such as climate change, the production and distribution of food, the supply of water, or pandemic diseases—even if they are not scientists or engineers themselves. The capacity to see connections across disciplines and contexts and to understand how scientists think will help students at each stage grasp scientific ideas that will be useful to them in their everyday lives long after they finish school.

---

[3]Two National Research Council reports provide more information about research on learning: *How People Learn: Brain, Mind, Experience, and School: Expanded Edition* (National Research Council, 2000), available at http://www.nap.edu/catalog/9853 [May 2016] and *How Students Learn: Science in the Classroom* (National Research Council, 2005), available at http://www.nap.edu/catalog/11102 [May 2016]. An update of *How People Learn* is forthcoming in 2017.

Science Learning Is Three-Dimensional

These insights about learning are reflected in a key idea laid out in the 2012 framework: namely, that science learning should be *three-dimensional*. Instruction that develops scientific thinking and learning will integrate three dimensions: (1) the *practices* through which scientists and engineers do their work; (2) the *crosscutting concepts* that apply across science disciplines; and (3) the *core* ideas of the disciplines.[4] What are these three dimensions?

Scientific and Engineering Practices

Scientists and engineers rely on eight key practices, such as asking questions and defining problems, planning and carrying out investigations, and analyzing and interpreting data. These are called practices—not skills—because *when* and *why* a practice is needed is just as important as *how* it is done. As students engage in these practices for themselves, they come to understand that science and engineering are creative processes of developing explanations and solutions. These practices are not isolated from core ideas; they are the means by which scientists investigate and build models and theories.

The eight key practices are:

1. Asking questions (science) and defining problems (engineering)

2. Developing and using models

3. Planning and carrying out investigations

4. Analyzing and interpreting data

5. Using mathematics and computational thinking

6. Constructing explanations (science) and designing solutions (engineering)

7. Engaging in argument from evidence

8. Obtaining, evaluating, and communicating information

Students cannot master these practices without opportunities to directly experience them. When students have the opportunity to "do" science, they don't

---

[4]The 2012 framework describes the three dimensions in detail. The NGSS describe grade-level performance expectations associated with these three dimensions. The easiest way to see how the three dimensions work together is to explore the NGSS website: http://www.nextgenscience.org [July 2016]. The description of these NGSS ideas in this book closely follows the text of the report on which this book is based, *Developing Assessments for the Next Generation Science Standards*.

just learn facts and ideas; they learn to engage in complex scientific reasoning. By "doing" the practices students also demonstrate how they are thinking through a challenge and provide opportunities for educators to assess what they are learning. As the quick look at student scientists at work shown in Box 1-1 demonstrates, teaching students to do science for themselves can be messy but can help them develop a love for science.

BOX 1-1 STUDENTS DOING SCIENCE

Jazmine . . . set up a jar to investigate a question about the growth of aquatic plants. The substrate [material the plants were rooted in] chosen . . . was gravel. After four weeks of observation and data collection, Jazmine noticed that another group had used soil as their substrate. Her experiences suggested that soil would be a better substrate (all the plants she saw on land grew in soil). Yet, the plants in her jar were thriving, while those grown in soil [were] not. In fact, the other group's question had shifted to trying to identify reasons for the continuing demise of their plants, which, in turn led to the death of their animals (ghost shrimp and daphnia). Jazmine speculated that [the answer] had something to do with nutrients provided by the substrate. She decided to set up three jars, identical in plants, animals, and environment, and differing only in substrate. She was no longer interested in the original question. She now had enough experience and understanding of aquatic environments and interactions to see an anomaly: Plants should grow better in soil than gravel because there should be more nutrients available, but the opposite was happening. Jazmine needed time to detect patterns, make connections, and notice anomalies.

SOURCE: Lucas et al. (2005). Reprinted with permission from the National Science Teachers Association.

Crosscutting Concepts

Some scientific concepts are important within and across disciplines. Crosscutting concepts are important tools for making sense of phenomena that can be observed. They help students structure their thinking about new observations and information they encounter and provide a scaffold upon which they can build understanding. These ideas—such as "cause and effect," "systems and system models," and "energy and matter"—help students make connections across contexts and over time. The crosscutting concepts are:

- *Patterns*. Observed patterns of forms and events guide organization and classification and prompt questions about relationships and the factors that influence them.

- *Cause and effect: mechanism and explanation.* Events have causes, sometimes simple, sometimes multifaceted. A major activity of science is investigating and explaining causal relationships and the mechanisms by which they are mediated. Such mechanisms can then be tested across given context and used to predict and explain events in new contexts.

- *Scale, proportion, and quantity.* In considering phenomena, it is critical to recognize what is relevant at different measures of size, time, and energy and to recognize how changes in scale, proportion, or quantity affect a system's structure or performance.

- *Systems and system models.* Defining the system under study—specifying its boundaries and making explicit a model of that system—provides tools for understanding and testing ideas that are applicable throughout science and engineering.

- *Energy and matter: flows, cycles, and conservation.* Tracking fluxes of energy and matter into, out of, and within systems helps one understand the systems' possibilities and limitations.

- *Structure and function.* The way in which an object or living thing is shaped and its substructure determine many of its properties and functions.

- *Stability and change.* For natural and built systems alike, conditions of stability and determinants of rates of change or evolution of a system are critical elements of study.

Disciplinary Core Ideas

There are core ideas to learn in each of the main disciplines of science—the physical, life, and Earth and space sciences—and in engineering, technology, and applications of science. Students could never learn all the important knowledge in these fields, but learning the core ideas will prepare them to understand and evaluate new information they learn on their own. A few examples of core ideas are that all living things are made up of cells, that plants depend on water and light to grow, and that wind and water can change the shape of land.[5]

---

[5]Chapters 5–8 of *A Framework for K–12 Science Education* describe the core ideas in each field (National Research Council, 2012).

Core ideas for K–12 science:

- have broad importance across science and engineering fields or are key organizing ideas in a field;

- provide a key tool for understanding or investigating more complex ideas and solving problems;

- relate to students' life experiences and personal concerns; and

- can be taught and learned over multiple grades at increasing levels of depth and sophistication.

The core ideas fall under four broad areas of science:

Physical Sciences
    Matter and its interactions
    Motion and stability: Forces and interactions
    Energy
    Waves and their applications in technologies for information transfer
Life Sciences
    From molecules to organisms: Structures and processes
    Ecosystems: Interactions and variation of traits
    Heredity: Inheritance and variation of traits
    Biological evolution: Unity and diversity
Earth and Space Sciences
    Earth's place in the universe
    Earth's systems
    Earth and human activity
Engineering, Technology, and Applications of Science
    Engineering design
    Links among engineering, technology, science, and society

Integrating the Three Dimensions

The idea that these three elements of learning—practices, crosscutting concepts, and disciplinary core ideas—need to be woven through every aspect of science education, not taught as separate entities, is called *three-dimensional learning*. It is important to learn science this way because doing science requires multilayered thinking. The practices that scientists and engineers use are tools for collecting or making sense of data, testing a hypothesis, or in some way answering a question or solving a problem. Identifying which tools are needed and applying them is at the heart of doing science. Often it is the creativity of an experimental design or a way to collect information, or the originality of an approach to data analysis, that constitutes a scientific breakthrough. Scientists and engineers see how to apply

the practices they have mastered because of what they understand about crosscutting concepts and core ideas.

Rather than simply mastering what is on a list of important science skills, students need to learn to use the practices the ways scientists do: that is, applying them as they are needed to solve a problem. At the same time, students cannot fully understand scientific information and conclusions without some understanding of the methods scientists use to investigate, analyze, communicate, and draw conclusions about the subject. Students need to gradually build their understanding of crosscutting concepts and begin to see how they apply in different contexts. And students need to gradually build an understanding of how core ideas from one branch of science relate to others: for instance, how ideas from chemistry can help them understand what happens when the body digests food. Three-dimensional instruction teaches students to think like scientists and provides the foundation for them to develop sophisticated science reasoning skills.

Key Idea

Three-dimensional learning is not just important for the education of future scientists and engineers; it is essential to help all students understand how science works and how to use that understanding to learn, make decisions, and understand their world throughout their lives and in their careers as adults. It's a key aspect of the new vision for science learning.

Science Understanding Develops Gradually

When we see the purpose of science education as helping students learn to reason, ask questions, and test their ideas the way scientists and engineers do, it's a reminder that learning develops gradually over time. This is not a new idea: teachers know that students learn as they are ready to do so and that they need to continuously build on what they have already mastered. For decades researchers have also been exploring the way learning develops and have provided insights that are already strong influences on education in science and other subjects. These insights were a foundation for the development of the 2012 framework, the NGSS, and other standards that were based on the framework's vision for science learning.

Students have many ideas of their own that are not supported by scientific evidence. These ideas are generally grounded in experience and are starting points that teachers can work with to help students build more accurate and complete understanding. This is important on a daily basis in the classroom: Students may begin the study of, say, the solar system, with their own ideas about the orbits of the planets and other topics they are learning about. Teachers can uncover those ideas and use them to draw students into the ideas and activities they are teaching.

Understanding how students' understanding develops is also important in the longer term: Expectations for students in early elementary school are naturally quite different from those for high school students. What students can readily understand in elementary school will be simpler than what they are able to understand later. Recognizing the steps along the learning pathway, and having strategies to address them, allows teachers to use and build on them and, as students are ready, to address ideas that are not scientifically accurate.

Ideally, students will encounter crosscutting concepts and disciplinary core ideas in different ways in each of their science classes, in many different contexts. The sophistication of their understanding will grow as they use and apply them and gain facility with science practices in the course of countless science experiences. This kind of learning requires coordination, or what educators call *coherence*, across disciplines and across students' years of schooling.

Coherence

Science education that helps students develop requires careful coordination of all its elements, or coherence. For a science education program to be coherent:

- instruction, curriculum, and assessments, as well as professional development and other key elements, must all be aligned to the same learning objectives and work together to support student learning; and

- learning goals (performance expectations) and curriculum must be aligned across all the years of science education so that the instruction in each year builds on—rather than repeats—what came before and prepares students well for what comes after.

One key to coherence is the way goals for learning, or performance expectations, are defined. These are descriptions of what students are expected to be able to do and understand. The performance expectations in the NGSS are targets for assessment, and they describe how students can demonstrate their ability to understand and use their knowledge (crosscutting concepts and disciplinary core ideas) through engaging in science and engineering practices. Other standards that are using the ideas in the framework also tie these aspects of learning together.

In a coherent science education system, performance expectations help guide each element so it supports students as they broaden their understanding of crosscutting concepts and core ideas and expand their facility with the practices of science and engineering. This is a collective responsibility, but you contribute to the coherence of your students' science education in many ways, as we discuss in Chapter 5.

Learning Progressions

Coherence is a general principle, but at its root are the expectations for student learning. The path toward mastery or expertise in a particular area can be called a learning progression. Researchers have examined learning for particular kinds of understanding in science and other subjects. For some topics they have described specific learning progressions that are typical for most students and thus can be used by educators to shape instruction. By explaining what students are expected to know and to be able to do, standards describe performance expectations for each level and each topic or area. Standards that reflect three-dimensional learning include explicit descriptions of how the understanding of crosscutting concepts and core ideas, as well as facility with practices, develops over time. Students will develop an understanding of knowledge and concepts by engaging in practices that help them question and explain what they observe.

Newer standards such as the NGSS reflect the importance of the learning process. They make clear both that students should be encouraged to use what they know in reasoning about what they observe and that struggling is critical to learning, just as it is a critical part of the way science is done.

The example in Box 1-2 shows a learning progression from the NGSS. Researchers have developed descriptions like these for some science topics, but not all are based on empirical research; others are hypothetical.

BOX 1-2 LEARNING PROGRESSION FOR FOOD IDEAS

Grades K–2: Animals obtain food they need from plants or other animals. *Plants need water and light.*

Grades 3–5: Food provides animals with the materials and energy they need for body repair, growth, warmth, and motion. *Plants acquire material for growth chiefly from air, water, and process matter and obtain energy from sunlight,* which is used to maintain conditions necessary for survival.

Grades 6–8: *Plants use the energy from light to make sugars through photosynthesis.* Within individual organisms, food is broken down through a series of *chemical reactions that rearrange molecules and release energy.*

Grades 9–12: The *hydrocarbon backbones of sugars produced through photosynthesis are used to make amino acids* and other molecules that can be assembled into proteins or DNA. Through cellular respiration, matter and energy flow through different organizational levels of an organism as elements are recombined to form different products and transfer energy. Cellular respiration is a key mechanism to release the energy an organism needs.

SOURCE: NGSS Lead States (2013, Appendix E). Copyright 2013 Achieve, Inc. All rights reserved.

This NGSS learning progression describes stages in understanding that are natural and expected: what students learn in the earlier grades is not wrong, but it is less complete than what they learn later. A big difference across the stages is seen in how crosscutting concepts and core disciplinary ideas are woven in. The phrases in italics in the learning progression in Box 1-2 show how ideas become more sophisticated over time—each building on the strong foundation established in earlier years. This happens when the curriculum and instruction are coherent across time, and teachers are aware both of the ways their students have encountered these ideas before and of how they will continue to develop later.

As we will see in later chapters, this idea is the key to assessing three-dimensional learning as it is described in the 2012 framework. The assessments we will explore demonstrate ways of collecting evidence about how students are progressing along a pathway that leads to the three-dimensional performance expectations, whether for a lesson, a unit, or a grade level.

Key Idea

The idea that student learning develops gradually and cumulatively fits perfectly with a three-dimensional approach to learning: this kind of understanding can come only through repeated opportunities to do science across units, disciplines, and years. The goals for units and stages of growth describe what can be expected of students at a particular stage; they are also stepping stones for the more sophisticated and complex understanding students will be capable of as they integrate crosscutting concepts with disciplinary core ideas, using their developing expertise with science and engineering practices. New science standards and curricula are designed so that students encounter concepts and practices as they are ready for them; the concepts and practices become more elaborate as students grow and gain experience.

CHANGES IN THE CLASSROOM

The idea of three-dimensional science learning can sound abstract, but it translates into immediate practical changes in instruction in the classroom. Teachers who are responding to this vision are shifting their focus. Rather than concentrating on helping students absorb sets of factual knowledge, the teacher can focus on strengthening students' capacity to think and reason about the ideas and information they are tackling. Students who learn this way gradually expand the breadth of their understanding of crosscutting concepts and core ideas as they gain mastery at posing and investigating scientific questions and analyzing their findings. This shift in focus is expressed in many changes large and small in daily classroom practice, such as the ones listed in Table 1-1.

These differences in classroom practice also reflect the idea that learning develops gradually and cumulatively. Notice that the activities in the right-hand column tend to be ones that take time, may be done in multiple steps, and involve many different types of tasks. These activities also allow the students to direct their own learning—pursuing their ideas and hypotheses within an instructional structure rather than simply following instructions. Many are also activities that can be done with different degrees of sophistication at different grade levels.

TABLE 1-1 Changes in Classroom Practice

Less of This	More of This
Rote memorization of facts and terminology	Facts and terminology learned as needed while students are developing explanations and designing solutions supported by evidence-based arguments and reasoning, in the context of crosscutting concepts and core ideas
Learning of ideas disconnected from questions about phenomena	Learning of core knowledge focused on explaining phenomena and understanding context for the ideas and information, using crosscutting concepts
Teachers providing information to the whole class	Students conducting investigations, solving problems, and engaging in discussions with teachers' guidance to trace connections to crosscutting concepts and core ideas
Teachers posing questions with only one right answer	Students discussing open-ended questions that focus on the strength of the evidence used to generate claims and the significance of the ideas
Students reading textbooks and answering questions at the end of the chapter	Students reading multiple sources, including science-related magazine and journal articles and Web-based resources; students developing explanations that summarize what they've read and answer key questions
"Cook-book" laboratories or hands-on activities with pre-planned outcomes	Multiple investigations driven by students' questions with a range of possible outcomes that collectively lead to multiple explanations or arguments about outcomes
Worksheets	Students writing journals and reports; creating posters and media presentations that explain, argue, and elaborate on ideas related to performance expectations
Oversimplification of activities for students who are perceived to be less able to do science and engineering	Providing supports so that all students can engage in sophisticated science and engineering practices, applying them in answering science questions

SOURCE: Adapted from National Research Council (2015).

Capitalizing on Students' Natural Curiosity

One way to engage students in active science thinking—and help them to see connections and to understand how and why science ideas are important—is called "anchoring instruction in a phenomenon." With this approach, the teacher identifies a phenomenon—a puzzling or counterintuitive circumstance, event, or process—that is apparent to her students. A phenomenon might be an unusual weather pattern, the behavior of animals that students observe on a field trip, or questions students have about how a particular technology works. The teacher challenges the students to explain or resolve it or to design a solution to a problem. Often the teacher is responding to what students notice and ask about, and he or she uses that opportunity to structure instruction, as the second-grade teacher in the example at the beginning of the chapter did when her students noticed changes in the corn.

This teacher identified an opportunity that was not only fun and interesting but also engaged students' genuine curiosity about something that can be explained scientifically. Furthermore, the science needed to explain this phenomenon was part of the learning objectives for the class, so the teacher could use what the students noticed about the corn to move learning forward in a purposeful way.

Wherever a teacher finds it, a well-chosen phenomenon will focus the students on connections between what they are learning and what they observe in the world. It will provide the students with a shared experience to which they all have equal access. It will require the students to integrate different science or engineering ideas and practices in order to collect the evidence and other information they need to meet the challenge. Students will draw on what they already know and use the practices they have at their command to explore further.

A phenomenon or problem that would work well for instruction will[6]:

- build on everyday experiences and relate to things students do or recognize. It's especially important that it engages students from varied cultural and language backgrounds.

- relate to performance expectations, engaging students in core ideas and cross-cutting concepts and requiring them to use science and engineering skills.

- be too complex for students to solve in a single lesson. The possible solutions should be ones that students could not find online or reach without some teacher guidance.

- be observable to students. The phenomenon should be something students can learn more about by, for example, using scientific procedures or technological devices such as telescopes or microscopes, collecting data outside, or finding patterns in data.

---

[6]These ideas are drawn from material posted by the R+P Collaboratory; see http://stemteachingtools.org/assets/landscapes/STEM-Teaching-Tool-28-Qualities-of-Anchor-Phenomena.pdf [May 2016]. For more ideas about activities that are engaging to students in this way, as well as instructional materials, see other practice briefs at http://stemteachingtools.org/brief/26 [April 2016] and the resources at http://ngss.nsta.org [May 2016].

- be something students can learn more about with data, images, and text that are accessible to them. It should allow them to use science and engineering practices to conduct firsthand or secondhand investigations.

- be a specific set of circumstances, such as a case or a problem (e.g., an infestation of pine beetles), or something that puzzles the students (e.g., why isn't rainwater salty?), or something students wonder about (e.g., how did the solar system form?).

- is important. The phenomenon should be a problem or question that people care about so the students will clearly see why their findings are important.

In one example of this approach, developed by the Inquiry Hub, the phenomenon to be explained is the planting of trees in cities—an activity that is intended to be beneficial to the environment but, in many cases, actually disrupts the local ecosystem.[7] The students are asked to figure out what kinds of trees should be planted, and where, to maximize the intended benefits. They can then do a series of investigations to explain such specific questions as How do trees affect an ecosystem and its habitats and food web? and What trade-offs are involved when trees are planted? They are given the challenge of choosing a species of tree to plant in their schoolyard that would be optimal for promoting biodiversity as well as benefits to human beings and other organisms.

Engaging Students from Diverse Backgrounds

Science educators are aware of the importance of respecting students' diverse experiences and cultural backgrounds and using them in instruction. All students bring valuable life experience and ideas to their classrooms, and their science learning is most successful when instruction draws on and connects with that richness. Because science involves specialized language, as well as the precise use of words and ideas that are understood more loosely outside the science context, English-language learners have an extra challenge in the science classroom. It can also be challenging for educators, who must bear these issues in mind along with the many other goals they have for their teaching practice.

A key idea in the 2012 framework is that science is critical for all students. The varied science activities that allow students to develop three-dimensional

---

[7]The example, developed by Sam Severance, can be found at http://learndbir.org/resources/2-NSELA-2015-Tools-for-NGSS-aligned-Unit-Development.pdf [May 2016]. See http://www.inquiryhub.org [May 2016] for more information about Inquiry Hub.

understanding provide many entry points for students as well as opportunities for educators to elicit and connect with their experiences. Students learning this way can demonstrate their understanding in a variety of ways, and teachers working this way can take advantage of phenomena that capture their students' imaginations.

Key Ideas

Teachers who are teaching in a three-dimensional way will structure student-centered instruction that

▶ weaves together a wide variety of science practices with learning about important crosscutting concepts and disciplinary core ideas;

▶ is flexible, allowing students to explore as they pursue learning objectives;

▶ works cumulatively, helping students develop their understanding over time, and provides continuous support at all stages of the learning process;

▶ engages students in investigating phenomena from everyday life;

▶ recognizes that learning requires repeated engagement with important ideas, guidance, and opportunities for reflection; and

▶ provides all students with avenues to science learning.

A NEW WAY TO THINK ABOUT ASSESSMENT

What exactly do all these changes mean for assessment? All assessments are intended to support teaching and learning by collecting information about what students know and can do. As teachers move to teaching in a three-dimensional way, focusing on learning over time, they will need to collect different kinds of information.

To measure three-dimensional learning that develops over time, assessments need to:

- examine how students use science and engineering practices in the context of crosscutting concepts and disciplinary core ideas;

- use a variety of tasks and challenges to give students multiple opportunities and ways to demonstrate what they have learned;

- provide diverse and specific information that shows teachers where students are struggling in their learning and helps them decide on next steps; it also helps students understand the progress they have made and where they need to go next; and

- focus on students' progress along a learning pathway rather than what is correct or incorrect at a particular time.

Teachers will want to use assessments that accomplish these goals to support their own teaching, but it will be just as important that other kinds of science assessments be developed with the same goals in mind. Ideally, next-generation classroom assessments will need to be part of assessment systems in which all the components are also designed to measure three-dimensional learning that develops over time. This will not happen right away, of course, and teachers are sometimes caught in the middle as large changes such as these develop. Regardless of how quickly districts and states develop such assessment systems, the change will begin with classroom assessment, and there is much that an individual educator can do.

Assessment in the Classroom

Performance expectations that reflect the 2012 framework, whether for curriculum units or for grade levels, are not descriptions of isolated concepts or skills students are expected to master by a particular point in time. Instead, they describe how students are expected to make connections among practices, crosscutting concepts, and disciplinary core ideas and to show how they have built on the understanding they developed in an earlier unit or grade. This means that assessments should not focus on isolated ideas or skills either. They should provide evidence of students' developing capabilities and insight into their partially correct or incomplete understanding—they should help teachers "see" their students' learning. Assessments that accomplish this will have multiple components and be constructed so they can provide information about this kind of multidimensional learning.

Without a doubt, this is a big change, but the three-dimensional assessment you do in your classroom can be an important contribution to the process. What you do in the classroom starts with the performance expectations for the grade and the subject you are teaching. Whether your school is using the NGSS or other standards that support three-dimensional science learning, you have learning goals for the year as well as more specific objectives. These objectives also drive when and how you assess your students' learning. You most likely already use many kinds of assessments to check on your students' progress because doing so is essential to good instruction.

As you adapt your instruction to the new vision of science learning, you will be finding many more ways to engage your students in doing science for themselves. The second-grade students who were investigating wet corn in the case at the beginning of the chapter were engaging in science practices from the start of their discussions. They raised scientific questions based on their observations. They collected evidence and attempted to explain the evidence, and they engaged in argumentation to compare competing ideas and reach consensus. This class investigation demonstrates how different types of activities can provide natural opportunities for assessment. As you gain experience with new approaches to

assessment, you will be able to use classroom activities to collect new kinds of information about what your students are learning and to use new strategies to gain insight from your assessments.

For example, when your students are developing and using models, you can observe how they explain and discuss them with classmates. Their discussion can give you a window into their thinking and help you make instructional decisions. To assess your students' progress toward learning objectives, you may use material they produce as a part of such classroom activities, such as lab reports or data displays, or choices they make using a computer-based activity rather than tests or quizzes.

These and other activities are all ways students can show you what they understand and give you clues about where they need help while they are actively engaged in doing science. You may not necessarily have thought of all these sorts of activities as assessment opportunities, but the information they provide can become an integral part of your instruction.

Assessment as a System

The assessments you use in the classroom—whether they are tests, quizzes, or other activities, and whether you developed them or are using assessments that are part of your instructional materials—are closely linked to the instructional activities you are doing. Your students most likely also take tests developed by your district or state that address the content you are covering but may not reflect the specific content you were teaching before they were given.

Ideally, the assessments you use in your classroom will be reinforced by the other kinds of assessments used in your district and state. While this would be the hope with all assessments, districts and states can develop systems for science assessment that are purposefully coordinated. In this kind of system[8]:

- all assessments are truly linked to instruction and curriculum so that each one is measuring—and reinforcing—what and how students are really taught; and

- all assessments work together—so that regardless of their purpose they reflect the same vision of how students learn science.

The idea of an assessment system begins with a commonsense point: no one assessment—or assessment occasion—can meet all the needs for information about what students know and can do in science. The purpose of collecting assessment information is to use it in some way to benefit students, but the different people involved in science education will use information in different ways. For example, parents need to have an accurate understanding of what teachers are doing in the classroom, and of what students are expected to do to graduate, so they can provide effective support for their children. Administrators use assessment data to evaluate programs and monitor how the students in their school are progressing. Policy makers use it to monitor larger groups, and the public uses it to hold the school system accountable for the education it is providing.

Even though the uses are different, the questions teachers who are integrating the three dimensions of science learning will ask about their students' progress are the same ones that can provide a meaningful picture of how well the students are mastering the standards. This is exactly the information that policy makers who monitor learning on a larger scale want, even though they need to look across much larger numbers of students. They will also want to know whether students have equitable opportunities to learn and do science—and here, also, the answers are found in the classroom.

---

[8]For a detailed discussion of systems for state science assessment, see National Research Council (2006).

This approach is different from the way most states have traditionally assessed science learning, but many states were thinking about taking a systems approach to their science assessments even before the 2012 framework for science learning was put forward. In the past, the goal has been to align instruction, curriculum, and assessment with standards. That's still just as important, but in a systems approach, the focus is not only on aligning each piece with a central set of content standards but also on the ways each part of the system contributes to the others. In an assessment system, different types of information are collected throughout the year using a variety of assessment tools, but each type of information contributes to a bigger picture of student learning.

The results of each type of assessment will complement the results of others. This doesn't mean that all assessments will be explicitly linked, however; it does mean that each assessment is designed to measure learning of the three-dimensional performance objectives being taught in the classroom. Different assessments—components of the system—will provide different kinds of information that can be used for different purposes.

It is important to be clear that this will be a complicated transition for states and districts. Developing and implementing such a system poses practical and political challenges that will take time to solve. Most districts and states are likely to make these changes gradually, and educators will need to adapt as materials, external tests (those developed outside the classroom and the school), and other elements evolve. Changing large-scale accountability tests may be the most challenging piece of the puzzle, but teachers can proceed even while system-wide changes are evolving. Chapter 5 talks further about the parts of an assessment system and the role individual teachers can play in fostering these changes. Here we focus on the specific changes in assessments that enable them to measure the development of three-dimensional science learning.

What Will Be Different?

Adaptation to three-dimensional science learning will mean changes in every type of assessment, guided by a few key ideas:.

Assessment Is Grounded in the Classroom

Three-dimensional assessment for any purpose has to be grounded in what takes place in the classroom: that is, in the curriculum and the way it is taught. The classroom assessments you use are not an intrusion into what you do; they are an integral part of your teaching because you want information about what your students know and can do. The information you collect this way is essentially the same sort of information any science assessment should collect: evidence of what and how well students are learning and understanding. As the three-dimensional approach gets worked into teachers' practice, curriculum materials, instructional objectives, and professional development, assessments used for any purpose will need to capture this sort of learning if they are to provide meaningful information.

Assessments Should Be Linked to Everything Else

Instruction, curriculum, and assessment must be tightly linked—coherent—if they are to successfully address learning that builds over time. This sort of linkage has always been important, but aligning each element to a set of written standards is not enough. The three dimensions of science learning—practices, crosscutting concepts, and disciplinary core ideas—need to play a part in everything teachers and students do in science class. And they need to be woven together in a way that builds cumulatively.

Ideally, science education is a seamless system made up of several smaller systems. The systems that guide instruction, curriculum, and assessment will evolve together toward the new vision of learning, though in the real world this is not likely to happen in a seamless way. If you are ready to teach in the multidimensional way, but your school and district are still using traditional curriculum and materials, you will need to adapt gradually. As systems take shape, though, it will be critical to remember that if you give students who've been exposed to three-dimensional instruction a traditional assessment it won't provide you with strong information about their three-dimensional learning. When the systems are all grounded in the same model of how students' learning will develop across the years of schooling, they will all reinforce one another.

Assessments Should Work Together

Teachers want immediate information about how their own students are doing today. Administrators and district and state staff need information about larger groups of students and often across longer time periods. Each of these three parties needs the same *kind* of information: what and how well students have learned *in the classroom*. Just as science education should be a seamless system, so should science assessment. If all assessments are designed with the same vision of how students learn science in mind, then the information they collect will fit together—and can be used more effectively. The information from large-scale assessments will reflect what students have been doing in their classrooms and provide information that teachers can use to make instructional decisions.

And, information collected in the classroom itself can be standardized and used in new ways by administrators and district and state leaders.

In an assessment system designed to collect information about three-dimensional science learning, a range of types of assessments, given at different times and for different purposes, provides a corresponding range of information about students' learning and thinking. These varied, but related, assessments give the students themselves, as well as teachers, parents, administrators, and others, the information they need about the progress of science learning. They also contribute to a more detailed portrait of student learning than any one type of assessment by itself could provide. As you adapt your use of assessments, you will contribute to the building of that kind of system in your district and state.

In other words, large-scale assessments can provide information that is useful beyond the classroom but still measure the learning that takes place within it. These sorts of assessments may be designed to provide evidence about programs or individual students, but they can be designed to measure the learning in the same way classroom assessments are. Large-scale assessments, particularly the yearly tests used by districts and states, play a key role in shaping both expectations for student learning and public discussion and perceptions of science education. Therefore, it is critical that these tests be adapted along with instruction.

These changes are just beginning. Most of the science assessments that districts and states have been using were developed before the new vision for science learning—especially three-dimensional learning—were put forward. The idea of learning progressions has become well known, but it has rarely been used in the development of science assessments, especially the large-scale ones given to all students in a state. Even though many testing programs have included innovative ways to assess practices and complex concepts, they were not designed with three-dimensional learning in mind. States are just beginning to respond to these ideas, but California's CA-NGSS Summative Assessment Plan is one example of a large-scale assessment program that is based on the 2012 science framework.[9]

Opportunity to Learn Is Key

Ideally instruction, curriculum, materials, and assessment would all be adapted at the same time, but in the real world that may not happen. As you adapt your own assessment practices, it will be important to think about the opportunities

---

[9]For more information about this assessment program, see http://www.classroomscience.org/cde-reveals-and-state-board-approves-californias-ngss-summative-assessment-design-plan [April 2016] and http://www.cde.ca.gov/be/ag/ag/yr16/documents/mar16item02slides.pdf [April 2016]. The New York state grade 8 intermediate assessments are another example; see http://www.nysedregents.org/grade8/science/home.html [May 2016].

and resources your students have access to. Information about what students have had the opportunity to learn helps you—and other people in the system—do your best to give students equitable opportunities to learn science. But it also provides a check on what conclusions can be drawn from any assessment results. You know, for instance, that quizzing a student on material from a lesson he or she missed doesn't give you useful information.

Opportunity to learn doesn't just mean that the materials and curriculum were available; it means that all of the students had genuine access to the kind of instruction and learning the new standards envision. It is not fair to judge a student, a teacher, or a school for poor test performance if the students did not have true access to the learning described in the standards being assessed. Many factors could limit students' access to learning: Some are practical, such as a lack of resources, teachers who have not received necessary training and professional development, or insufficient time allotted for science learning. Other factors are more subtle, such as unrecognized assumptions about what will be familiar to students, or a reliance on communication styles that students are not comfortable with, which might impede their learning.

Teachers know their students best. Your students likely bring a mix of prior educational successes as well as challenges. Each one brings a cultural background and experiences that could influence their responses and contributions to the activities in your classroom. These experiences can be resources for learning. As you get to know a new group of students, you pay attention to students whose first language is not English to see whether their language skills will affect their understanding. You consider whether prior educational experiences, disabilities, or other factors will influence any of your students' learning.

Assessing students' opportunity to learn is also especially important while districts and states are gradually adapting their science education systems. This is because the jurisdictions cannot be sure how successfully a program or curriculum is performing without knowing about students' real access to the new approaches. District and state assessment and accountability systems should include ways to assess opportunity to learn, including documentation of instructional materials and instructional time, questionnaires for students and teachers, and classroom observations. But teachers are in the best position to report on changes they are making in their own classrooms because they know firsthand the experiences their students are having.

Key Idea

Assessments that measure three-dimensional science learning are integral to instruction because they allow the teacher to see how students are progressing. As districts and states adapt the NGSS-based approach to science education, all science assessments will need to be designed to measure three-dimensional learning that develops over time, and to work together as a system. Each kind of assessment will complement the others to build a composite picture of students' science learning—the system will also track students' access to three-dimensional science learning.

BUILDING ON ASSESSMENT BASICS—A QUICK PRIMER

These principles for designing new kinds of assessments build on good assessment practice: that is, the ground rules of psychometrics established over decades still apply. Each of the examples in this book illustrates a way to answer new kinds of questions about students' learning while still making sure the results support valid and reliable inferences about what students know and can do. In an assessment context, validity and reliability have very specific meanings[10]:

- People often describe tests as valid or not valid, but it is the interpretation of a test's results that must be shown to be valid. The process of validation involves collecting related evidence to support each particular interpretation or use of a test. For example, districts use scores on end-of-year subject matter tests (e.g., large-scale accountability tests) to report the percentage of students who are "proficient." Validity evidence to support this interpretation should include evidence that the test scores relate to other measures of achievement from that same school year, such as performance on end-of-course exams, or course grades.

- Reliability refers to the degree to which scores are consistent when a test is given at different times or under different conditions. For example, a reliability measure might indicate the extent to which student performance on two different administrations of a test will produce similar scores or the extent to which ratings of student work given by different judges are consistent. In other words, a rating of test reliability is an estimate of the extent to which the test scores are precise, free of random measurement error, and reproducible.

Assessment of any sort is a way of gathering and evaluating information, and in that way, it is like a scientific investigation. As in a science investigation, you have to identify the precise questions you want to answer, design a way to collect data to answer these questions, and design a structure for interpreting your results. To be useful, the individual tasks need to generate the information you want and need—not some other, irrelevant information. They need to generate results that you can interpret accurately and fairly, and you need to have confidence that they can reliably answer your questions even when the assessment is given on different days with different groups of students.

Here are some basic considerations to keep in mind as you adapt your approach to assessment. Our focus is on assessments you use in the classroom, but these principles apply to any type of assessment.

---

[10]Professional standards for the ethical and technical requirements of tests, including reliability and validity, are described in the *Standards for Educational and Psychological Testing* (2014). The National Council for Measurement in Education provides an online glossary of important testing-related terms at http://www.ncme. org/ncme/NCME/Resource_Center/Glossary/NCME/Resource_Center/Glossary1.aspx?hkey=4bb87415-44dc-4088-9ed9-e8515326a061 [October 2016].

The Purpose for Assessing Drives the Design

Science assessment systems are needed because people want information about student learning for many different reasons. Some assessments—such as statewide tests usually given once per year—are used to monitor large groups of students. Chapter 5 talks more about this type of assessment, but there are other reasons to assess in the classroom as well. The terms *formative* and *summative* assessment are commonly used to describe two primary purposes for assessing in the classroom. These terms refer to the way the results of an assessment are used—not to its design or characteristics.

Teachers use *formative* assessments to collect information they need to guide their instruction and that students need to improve their learning. A formative assessment might be as simple as a quick comprehension check, a pop quiz, a conversation with a student, or a classroom discussion. These kinds of assessments help teachers measure their students' progress and figure out what steps are needed to support them. They also help students understand explicitly what the criteria are for high-quality work and what they need to accomplish to meet expectations.

So, formative assessments might be used to:

● check on individual students' understanding of what you are teaching,

● get insight into students' thinking about science concepts and identify misunderstandings,

● make decisions about reteaching material or pacing the instruction, or

● help students evaluate and revise their own work.

Summative assessments are used at the end of a unit or a course to provide evidence of learning that can be used to make decisions such as assigning grades. They may be tests and exams designed by teachers, the results of which are used by them and their students. The large-scale assessments given by the district or state are also summative. Parents, school administrators, district or state officials, or others responsible for making sure that students progress as they should, use the results of these kinds of tests in making decisions.

Summative assessments provide results that can be used for purposes such as:

● assigning grades to individual students;

● informing parents about their children's progress;

- determining whether an individual student is ready for the next grade, or has performed well enough to graduate from high school;

- providing evidence of how students within a group have performed with respect to general levels of mastery, perhaps identified through research on learning progressions—such as "basic," "proficient," or "advanced";

- providing evidence of how well a group of students has performed in comparison with other groups—for example, fourth-grade students in a school or district as compared with those across their state; or

- providing evidence of how well a change—such as a revised curriculum, a new approach to professional development, or some other policy—has worked.

Just like formative assessments, summative ones should focus on three-dimensional learning and be closely linked both to the curriculum being taught and to specific performance expectations. What makes an assessment formative or summative is what you plan to do with the results. This means that planning for how results will be interpreted and how they will be communicated to the people who need them should be part of the design of the assessment from the beginning.

One Assessment Cannot Serve All Purposes

The purpose for which you need information should drive the design of the assessment you will use to collect that information. If you use an assessment for a purpose other than the one for which it was designed, the results won't support valid answers to the questions you are asking about student learning. For example, a test that is designed at the district or state level to assess the understanding of a large group of students, such as all fourth graders, may not also provide information about the specific areas that an individual student needs to work on. Different people have different reasons for asking questions about student learning, and you also will have different purposes for testing in your classroom depending on what aspects of your students' learning you are focused on. You may want a spot check of comprehension or a picture of how well students have learned the material in a complex multi-week unit.

Many of the examples in this book do serve multiple purposes because they are made up of multiple different tasks, each of which is designed for a specific purpose. A few of the examples show how you might design a task so that it can be used for a formative purpose while the students are learning and then used again, perhaps in a modified form, when summative information is needed. But it is critical to think precisely about the purpose of each use of an assessment task.

The Assessment Should Measure What You Intend It to Measure

Imagine a task that is intended to measure students' understanding of, say, the water cycle and asks students to write an extended answer. Students who are actually well able to do what the task is supposed to measure—for example marshaling evidence to explain something they observed—may not be able to demonstrate that ability on this assessment because of limited writing skills. There are a few ways to avoid this problem. You can be very precise about what it is you want to measure and how students can demonstrate that they have the understanding and knowledge you are interested in. You can carefully review an assessment task to see whether it poses unnecessary challenges that are not relevant to what you are measuring. You can also develop alternate ways for students to respond to the task and allow them some choice. For example, they might create a table or graph showing their evidence, or draw and label a picture.

It Is Critical to Be Sure Students Understand What They Are Being Asked to Do

For your students to demonstrate what they understand and can do, they need to be sure what the expectations are. If the assessment tasks you use are grounded in your instruction, and resemble the sorts of activities your students have been doing in class, it's likely that your students will know what is expected. But it's important to think carefully about the guidance your students will need both about what they are expected to do when they are being assessed and about the kinds of results they are working toward. Your students can show you what they have learned when the tasks you use to measure learning are examples of the same sorts of tasks you've used in teaching.

The Assessment Tasks and Context Should Be Consistent If Groups of Students Are to Be Compared

Developers of large-scale assessments are very careful about standardizing testing conditions (such as time allowed or the use of calculators) so that the results are comparable and fair across schools or districts. You also might want to compare results across students or groups of students within your classroom or across classrooms in your school. To do that fairly, you need to be sure that all students are doing the same assessment task, even if they do it on different days. Likewise, you need to be sure that all of them have been given the same instructions. Many three-dimensional assessments will have students engaged in doing science—and won't just rely on paper-and pencil tasks—but it is still possible

to make these tasks consistent and even to standardize their administration for large-scale accountability purposes. You'll want to ensure that the conditions are consistent and that the guidance, resources, and support the students have access to as they do the activity are consistent. For example, in an assessment in which your students will work with living organisms it is important that all the students encounter comparable challenges. If the organisms have not been exposed to the same conditions or are not at the same stage of development at the start of the activity, the results may be affected by factors that have nothing to do with how much the student knows or can do.

The Assessment Situation Should Give Every Student a Fair Opportunity to Demonstrate What He or She Has Learned

Teachers may be concerned that these new kinds of tasks are more challenging than traditional ones. If you are wondering whether your students will do well, remember that diverse kinds of evidence can show capacities that may have remained hidden with traditional assessments. You can give them multiple modes for expressing what they know and can do. As you adapt your instruction, your students will also adapt. Ideas for making instruction more inclusive and accessible will be especially applicable as you adapt your assessments.

CHAPTER HIGHLIGHTS

- Three-dimensional science standards—the NGSS and others—are based on the idea that in order to become science literate, students need continuous opportunities to do science. Engaging in science for themselves will teach students how and why science and engineering really matter and how scientists and engineers do what they do.

- Instruction that develops scientific thinking and learning will integrate three dimensions: (1) the practices through which scientists and engineers do their work; (2) the crosscutting concepts that apply across science disciplines; and (3) the core ideas of the disciplines. Coherent instruction and curriculum will allow students to build increasingly complex understanding across their years of schooling.

- Assessment is an integral aspect of this new kind of instruction because teachers need regular information about students' developing capacity to integrate the three dimensions of science learning: the practices of science and engineering, crosscutting concepts, and disciplinary core ideas.

- Assessments can be designed to measure three-dimensional learning while still following established measurement principles. Assessments of this kind of learning will often look a great deal like classroom activities. Teachers can structure many kinds of science activities to collect information about their students' learning as it develops.

- Three-dimensional assessments provide more information about students' developing understanding than many traditional assessments can. This information will help guide your teaching and your students' learning.

- These new kinds of assessments may be used for formative purposes (to collect information a teacher needs to guide instruction and help students improve their learning) or summative purposes (to provide evidence of learning after, an instructional unit, a course, or a grade is complete).

The specific examples we explore in the following chapters illustrate how this new approach to assessment works.

2

What Does This Kind of Assessment Look Like?

Three-dimensional assessment is new and not many people are using it yet. Nevertheless, researchers and educators have been exploring ways to measure the science learning described in the 2012 framework. They've come up with ideas for assessing students of different ages, for different purposes, and using many kinds of activities and resources. Each of the examples in this book uses an approach developed by researchers and educators for this purpose. For each example included in this book we identify which practices, crosscutting concepts, and disciplinary core ideas are assessed, along with the grade level or levels targeted.[1]

In this chapter we begin with some examples that introduce how three-dimensional assessments work. They illustrate ways to use familiar types of science activities as assessments that successfully measure the development of active, engaged, three-dimensional science learning. The first example, "What Is Going on Inside Me?," is from a set of biology lessons for middle school students. It illustrates one of the most important ideas we've talked about: namely, that assessment needs to be grounded in classroom instruction because it assesses what students have learned from a series of activities that reflect the multiple dimensions of science learning. Then we compare two assessments that measure similar material—one traditional and the other designed to assess learning as it is described in the 2012 framework—to explore the differences.

---

[1]Most of the examples in this book appeared in the report on which it is based, *Developing Assessments for the Next Generation Science Standards*. The descriptions were adapted to emphasize the aspects of them that are of greatest interest to practitioners.

DISSECTING AN EXAMPLE

"What Is Going on Inside Me?" is a set of lessons about the human body designed for middle school students. Over the course of many weeks, students work through lessons that provide the building blocks they need in order to understand how the body's systems and cellular processes work together. The lessons include many different activities: collecting, recording, and analyzing data; reviewing research; writing about their conclusions; and more. These activities introduce the students to the way scientists collect evidence and use reason to analyze it, and then test their claims about what might be happening. Through these activities students also become familiar with this science vocabulary. At certain points in these lessons the students do tasks that are specifically designed to provide evidence about what they have learned. These activities are not separate tests, but activities that make sense in the sequence of what the students are doing. They are formative assessments that give the teacher and the students insights about how learning is progressing.

EXAMPLE **1** **What Is Going on Inside Me?**

Level — **Middle school**

Assesses — **PRACTICES**—Constructing explanations; Engaging in argument from evidence

CROSSCUTTING CONCEPTS—Energy and matter: Flows, cycles, and conservation

DISCIPLINARY CORE IDEAS—Matter and its interactions [PS1][a]; From molecules to organisms: Structures and processes [LS1]

This example introduces key features of assessments that are grounded in classroom instruction and measure three-dimensional learning that develops gradually: it engages students in activities as part of an instructional unit in which they use science to demonstrate their mastery of performance objectives.

[a]PS1 and LS1 are codes used in the Next Generation Science Standards to refer to specific disciplinary core ideas. These codes are provided for all the examples for readers who want to explore the standards in detail; see http://www.nextgenscience.org [August 2016].

The task we'll look at might seem like a fairly straightforward exercise in which students are asked to write about what they have learned from a series of activities. In the lesson that includes this task, students are asked to write about what they have learned from one series of activities within the unit, called "The Case of the Missing Oxygen." The students first explore what is entering and leaving the body when they breathe and then where the oxygen goes within the body and why. The activities guide them to make and test predictions, acquire and discuss new information, carry out experiments, and track what they are discovering about respiration.

After working through these activities over numerous class periods, the students are asked to write a response to this prompt:

> Solving the mystery: Inspector Bio wants to know what you have figured out about the oxygen that is missing from the air you exhale. Explain to her where the oxygen goes, what uses it, and why. Write a scientific explanation with a claim, sufficient evidence, and reasoning.

This writing task gives students the opportunity to reflect on what they have learned and how it fits together to answer a broad question about respiration and its function, using scientific reasoning. This task might seem like a fairly straightforward exercise, similar to familiar writing prompts, but it illustrates two critical new assessment goals: measuring three-dimensional science learning and measuring the development of understanding over time.

This Task Measures Three-Dimensional Learning

The goal of "What Is Going on Inside Me?" is not only for students to learn how humans—like other animals—get their energy from food but also for them to use evidence to explain that the release of this energy must involve a chemical reaction. As they move through the activities, students develop an explanation for how the body obtains energy and building materials from food. In doing these things, the students demonstrate three-dimensional learning.

As they work toward this explanation, students connect *core ideas* from several science disciplines. They draw on ideas from physics and chemistry (e.g., conservation of matter, transformation of energy, and chemical reactions) as they explore how animals convert matter into energy. The concept of how energy and matter cycle and flow is a tool for understanding the functioning of any system; thus, the students are also learning about a *crosscutting concept*. They also use several *practices*: asking questions, planning and investigating, and constructing an argument from evidence.

The writing task helps the teacher see how well students do at the three-dimensional task of pulling together ideas and practices they have learned across several lessons.

This Task Measures Understanding That Has Developed Gradually

In the course of multiple lessons, the students have investigated cell growth and what cells need to survive and have identified what materials can get into and out of a cell. They have worked step-by-step to collect evidence and build an argument for the explanation that food is broken down and transported through the body to all the cells, where a chemical reaction occurs that uses oxygen and glucose to release energy for the cells to use.

As the students progress through the lessons, they begin, with the teacher's guidance, to focus on tracking where the oxygen goes and how it is used. Using the science practice of data analysis, the students notice that increased activity in the body is associated with increased oxygen intake. As they trace the oxygen and the glucose, they begin to conclude that the food and oxygen are going to all the cells of the body and that that is where the energy is released. The teacher supports the students in figuring out that the only way the matter could be rearranged in the ways needed—and release the energy that the cells appear to be using to do their work—is through a chemical reaction.

Students will not be able to put together these arguments without understanding what they had learned earlier about energy and chemical reactions. The students have done experiments with osmosis in which they saw that both water and glucose could enter the cell. Experiments with yeast have shown them that cells could use the glucose for energy and growth and that this process releases waste in the form of carbon dioxide gas. The students have also established both that increased energy needs (such as physical activity) are associated with increased consumption of air and that exhaled air contains proportionally less oxygen than does the air in the room.

Using their data students have to work out a series of ideas that help them develop a logical explanation for what they have observed. The following ideas are hypotheses that the students develop and test:

- *Something must be going on in the body that uses food, somehow gets the matter to be used in growth, and gets the energy to be used for all body functions.*

- *The increased mass that organisms have as they grow must come from somewhere, so it must be from the food input to the body.*

- *The only way for the body to get energy is to get it from somewhere else, either through transfer or conversion of energy.*

- *For the mass provided by the food to be used, a chemical reaction must be taking place that rearranges the substances.*

- *There must be a chemical reaction going on to get the stored energy in the food into a form usable by the body.*

- *The oxygen that is shipped around the body along with the broken-down food must be being used in a chemical reaction to convert the stored energy in the food molecules.*

The students' responses to the writing exercise show the teacher how well students have put together their ideas to form a scientific explanation. Below is a typical response from an eighth-grade student. It demonstrates that the student could apply science ideas (about energy and matter) to explain the oxygen question (National Research Council, 2014, p. 42).

After being inhaled, oxygen goes through the respiratory system, then the circulation system or blood, and goes throughout the body to all the cells. Oxygen is used to burn the food the body needs and get energy for the cells for the body to use. For anything to burn, it must have energy and oxygen. To then get the potential energy in food, the body needs oxygen, because it is a reactant. When we burned the cashew, the water above it increased, giving it thermal energy and heating it up. Therefore, food is burned with oxygen to get energy.

A guide for scoring the task is shown in Box 2-1.

The scoring rubric describes standardized examples of increasingly strong three-dimensional understanding. This student's response shows that he or she has made partial progress toward the performance expectations in the unit. This response shows that the student understands that the food contains potential energy but cannot elaborate on how the chemical reaction converts the energy to a form cells can use. The response provides evidence that the student drew on what he or she learned from the activities in thinking through the way oxygen is used by the body.

> ## BOX 2-1 SCORING RUBRIC FOR ASSESSMENT TASK
>
> Solving the mystery: Inspector Bio wants to know what you have figured out about the oxygen that is missing from the air you exhale. Explain to her where the oxygen goes, what uses it, and why. Write a scientific explanation with a claim, sufficient evidence, and reasoning.
>
> **Level 0:** Missing or only generic reasons for survival (e.g., to breathe, for living)
>
> **Level 1:** Oxygen used to get energy or used with food for energy; no physical science mechanism presented to get energy
>
> **Level 2:** Oxygen used in a chemical reaction (or "burning") to get energy, but an incomplete description of the physical science ideas of matter and energy (e.g., "burns the oxygen" without mentioning food or glucose or "react with glucose" but no account of energy)
>
> **Level 3:** Full account, using physical science ideas, including both the matter and energy accounts—oxygen is combined in a chemical reaction with food or glucose that includes a conversion of the stored energy in food to forms usable by the cells
>
> SOURCE: Adapted from Krajcik et al. (2013).

EXAMPLE

1

▶ The assessment task—like the instruction of which it is a part—seamlessly blends the three dimensions of science learning.

▶ The task measures what students have come to understand through multiple activities, and it helps the teacher make sure that the students have the foundation they need to build on that learning later.

▶ The assessment is a natural part of the unit. Students may not necessarily think of the writing exercise as an assessment because the task is one they recognize as an important activity they do frequently to help them integrate their thinking about a phenomenon.

▶ The scoring rubric helps the teacher understand specifically where the students need more support or instruction.

▶ The standardized scoring rubric could be used to compare the understanding of students beyond a single classroom or school.

COMPARING A TRADITIONAL ASSESSMENT WITH THE NEW APPROACH

The next two assessment activities were chosen to highlight some of the differences between familiar assessment approaches and strategies that match the new vision of science learning. Both are assessments of similar material for upper elementary school students.

Traditional Example

First, let's look at a set of activities called "How Do Plants and Animals Depend on Each Other?" from a popular textbook for fourth-grade students (see Figure 2-1). The students create a terrarium, make observations about the organisms, and record measurements of their size at the start and 1 week later. The activities on the second page can be used to assess students' understanding of how the organisms depend on one another—the text in blue shows the expected accurate responses.

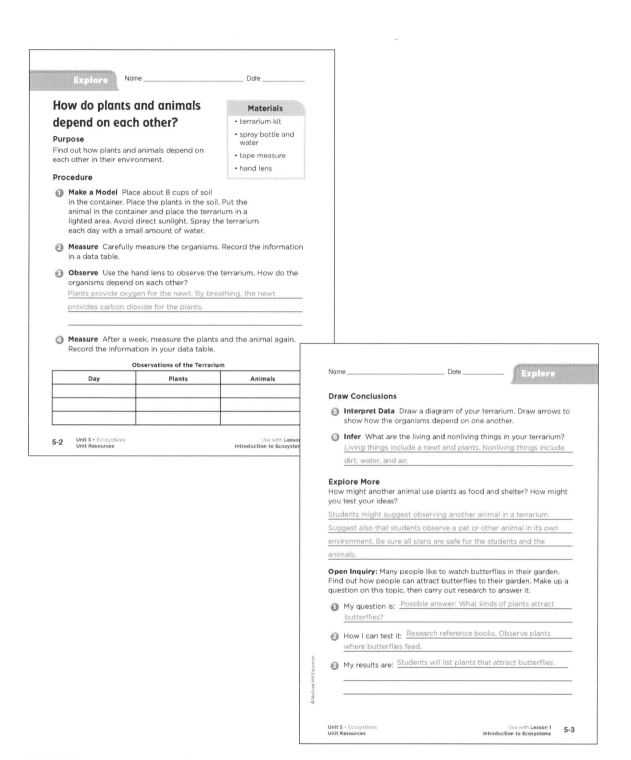

FIGURE 2-1 Assessment activities from a textbook.

SOURCE: McGraw-Hill Education (2008, pp. 5-2, 5-3). Reprinted with permission from McGraw-Hill Education.

Three-Dimensional Approach

Now compare this to the following set of activities designed to work together to assess fifth-graders' learning about biodiversity. This one was designed to capture the kind of learning described in the 2012 framework.

EXAMPLE **2** **Biodiversity in the Schoolyard**

Level   **Grade 5**

Assesses   **PRACTICES**—Planning and carrying out investigations; Analyzing and interpreting data; Constructing explanations

CROSSCUTTING CONCEPTS—Patterns

DISCIPLINARY CORE IDEAS—Biological evolution: Unity and diversity [LS4]

This example highlights key differences between a traditional assessment and one that can measure three-dimensional learning that develops over time. Not only does this activity engage students in doing science, it also uses a task in different ways—to teach and to assess.

"Biodiversity in the Schoolyard" is a set of four activities that are part of an extended unit in the same way the task we examined in "What Is Going on Inside Me?" was. In this unit, the students collect and analyze data about the various species living in the yard of their school. All of the activities they do are natural parts of the instructional sequence in the unit, but some are also designed to help the teacher see the students' progress. We will look at four activities that use multiple assessment strategies to collect different sorts of information about students' learning. These activities are three-dimensional. They focus on core disciplinary ideas associated with biodiversity: one, that it describes the variety of species found in Earth's terrestrial and oceanic systems, and two, that the completeness and integrity of an ecosystem's biodiversity is often used as a measure of its health. The crosscutting concept of patterns comes up as students explore these ideas using the practices of conducting an investigation, interpreting the data they collect, and developing explanations for what they have observed.

The following three assessment tasks are parts of an investigation the students carry out.

> Task 1: Students work in teams to collect data on the number of animals (abundance) and the number of different species (richness) they find in each of three zones within their schoolyard.

Instructions: Once you have formed your team, your teacher will assign your team to a zone in the schoolyard. Your job is to go outside and spend approximately 40 minutes observing and recording all of the animals and signs of animals that you see in your schoolyard zone during that time. Use the BioKIDS application on your iPod to collect and record all your data and observations.

In this example, students use an iPod to record the information they collect, but they could also use paper and clipboards to do the same thing. The data from each iPod are uploaded and combined into a spreadsheet that contains all the students' data, but the teacher and students could create the spreadsheet themselves. (A sample electronic spreadsheet is shown in Figure 2-2.) The teacher reviews the data to see how well the students collected and recorded the data, which they will need for the other tasks. The teacher can use the Internet interface to look at each group's data and also to look across data for all the students in the class.

Task 2: Students create bar graphs that illustrate patterns in the data showing abundance and richness of species for each of the schoolyard zones.

In the second task, students construct graphs of the data they have collected and then develop interpretations of what the data show. The exact instructions for Task 2 are shown in Figure 2-3. Teachers use the graphs the students create in deciding what further instruction students may need. For example, if students are having trouble drawing accurate bars or labeling the axes appropriately, a teacher can stop and focus instruction on those skills. The teachers also explain new vocabulary and concepts as needed. If the students are not showing a secure understanding of the core ideas—about species abundance or species richness—a teacher might review those before the students proceed.

Task 3: Students are asked to construct an explanation to support their answer to the question "Which zone of the schoolyard has the greatest biodiversity?"

This task functions as a learning exercise and a chance for the teacher to see how well students do at using their investigation and the data from the graphs they have developed as evidence to support their explanations. Before they start this task, the students will already have completed a separate activity (not an assessment) that helped them understand this definition of biodiversity: "An area is considered biodiverse if it has both a high animal abundance and high species richness."

Animal Name	Zone A	Zone C	Zone E	Microhabitat	Total
Earthworms	2	0	2	– In dirt	4
Ants	2	229	75	– On something hard – On grass	306
Other insects	0	0	2	– On grass – Other microhabitat	2
Unknown beetle	0	3	0	– On plant	3
Unknown insect	0	2	0	– On dirt	2
Other leggy invertebrates	1	0	0	– In dirt	1
American robin	6	1	3	– On tree – In the sky	10
Black tern	200	0	0	– On plant – On something hard	200
House sparrow	0	0	1	– On tree	1
Mourning dove	3	0	0	– On tree	3
Unknown bird	7	5	2	– On tree – In the sky	14
Other birds	0	1	2	– In water – On grass	3
E. fox squirrel	1	1	0	– On something hard	2
Human	10	21	1	– On grass – On something hard – Other microhabitat	32
Other mammal	3	0	16	– Other microhabitat – On something hard	19
Red squirrel	2	0	0	– On tree	2
Number of Animals (Abundance)	237	263	104		604
Number of Kinds of Animals (Richness)	11	8	9		28

FIGURE 2-2 Class summary of animal observations in the schoolyard, organized by region (schoolyard zones).
SOURCE: National Research Council (2014, p. 106).

Instructions:

1. Use your zone summary to make a bar chart of your **abundance** data.

Please remember to label your axes.

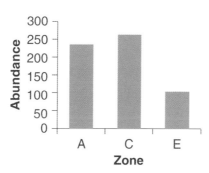

Our Abundance Data

Result: According to the bar chart above, **Zone C** has the highest abundance.

2. Use your zone summary to make a bar chart of your **richness** data.

Please remember to label your axes.

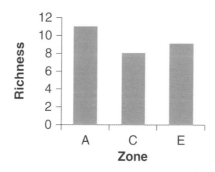

Our Richness Data

FIGURE 2-3 Instructions for Task 2.

SOURCE: National Research Council (2014, p. 107).

As they start to work on developing their explanations, the students are also given hints that there are three key parts of an explanation: a claim, more than one piece of evidence, and reasoning. The students are also given the definitions of relevant terms. This task allows the teacher to see how well students have understood the concept and can support their ideas about it using the practices of data analysis and explanation. It also gives students a chance to develop their own understanding through hints and some definitions that are tools they can use to construct their explanations. The students also gain practice pulling their ideas together into a scientific explanation with the three needed elements. Instructions for Task 3 and sample student answers are shown in Box 2-2.

The first three tasks are designed so they can function as learning activities while also providing the teacher with formative information she can use to shape instruction. The last task is designed to be given at the end of the entire unit to assess the students' understanding of the learning objectives regarding biodiversity and their capacity to reason scientifically about what they have learned. Results from Task 4 can be used in summative ways—as part of the students' recorded grades, for example.

> Task 4: Students are again asked to construct an explanation to support an answer to the question about which zone of the schoolyard has the greatest biodiversity, but this time without the supports the teacher provided the first time.

The teacher presents the students with excerpts from a class data collection summary (shown in Table 2-1) and asks them to construct an explanation, as they did in Task 3. Although this task is much the same as Task 3, it now is being used for a summative purpose. The difference between the two is that in Task 4, the hints are not given: at the end of the unit, the students are expected to show without assistance that they understand what constitutes a full explanation. The task and coding rubric used for Task 4 are shown in Box 2-3.

TABLE 2-1 **School Yard Animal Data**

Animal Name	Zone A	Zone B	Zone C	Total
Pillbugs	1	3	4	8
Ants	4	6	10	20
Robins	0	2	0	2
Squirrels	0	2	2	4
Pigeons	1	1	0	2
Animal Abundance	6	14	16	36
Animal Richness	3	5	3	5

SOURCE: National Research Council (2014, p. 110).

Instructions: Using what you have learned about biodiversity, the information from your class summary sheet, and your bar charts for abundance and richness, construct an explanation to answer the following scientific question:

Scientific Question: Which zone in the schoolyard has the highest biodiversity?
My Explanation [figure or text box?]

Make a CLAIM: Write a complete sentence that answers the scientific question.

Zone A has the greatest biodiversity.

> **Hint**
> Look at your abundance and richness data sheets carefully.

Give your REASONING: Write the scientific concept or definition that you thought about to make your claim.

Biodiversity is related to abundance and richness because it shows the two amounts in one word.

> **Hint**
> Think about how biodiversity is related to abundance and richness.

Give your EVIDENCE: Look at your data and find two pieces of evidence that help answer the scientific question.

1. *Zone A has the most richness.*
2. *Zone A has a lot of abundance.*

> **Hint**
> Think about which zone has the highest abundance and richness.

NOTES: Student responses are shown in italics. See text for discussion.

SOURCE: National Research Council (2014, p. 109).

BOX 2-3 TASK AND CODING RUBRIC FOR TASK 4 IN "BIODIVERSITY IN THE SCHOOLYARD"

Write a scientific argument to support your answer for the following question.

Scientific Question: Which zone has the highest biodiversity?

Coding

4 points: Contains all parts of explanation (correct claim, two pieces of evidence, reasoning)

3 points: Contains correct claim and two pieces of evidence but incorrect or no reasoning

2 points: Contains correct claim + one piece correct evidence OR two pieces correct evidence
          and one piece incorrect evidence

1 point: Contains correct claim, but no evidence or incorrect evidence and incorrect or no reasoning

Correct Responses

Claim

Correct: Zone B has the highest biodiversity.

Evidence

1. Zone B has the highest animal richness.
2. Zone B has high animal abundance.

Reasoning

Explicit written statement that ties evidence to claim with a reasoning statement i.e., Zone B has the highest biodiversity because it has the highest animal richness and high animal abundance. *Biodiversity is a combination of both richness and abundance*, not just one or the other.

SOURCE: National Research Council (2014, p. 111).

What Are the Differences?

We compare these two examples—the traditional and the three-dimensional one—not to suggest that the one in the textbook is of poor quality but to show different ways of working with similar material.

The "Biodiversity in the Schoolyard" assessment tasks are each three-dimensional: they are designed to engage students in a way that blends science practices with the crosscutting concepts and core ideas the unit is about. For example, the first task is structured to encourage the students to begin thinking about patterns in what they are finding as they collect their data—patterns is a crosscutting concept. The Internet interface reinforces ideas the class has discussed by guiding the students to think about how to structure the way they record their data (by zone of the schoolyard) and then in how to begin analyzing it (by creating bar graphs). These are elements of Practice 3: planning and carrying out investigations. As the students investigate the species in their schoolyard, they link what they are finding to the disciplinary core ideas their teacher has been introducing, about the richness and abundance of different species.

The Internet interface offers suggestions that help the students succeed. It also gives their teachers clear images of the understanding their students can demonstrate, as well as insights into where they fall short. The final task gives the students the opportunity to demonstrate different sorts of understanding they have developed in the course of the unit.

In contrast, the tasks in the textbook assessment (see Figure 2-1) each address something important, but they were not designed to address three-dimensional learning that develops over time. In Step 3, for example, the students are asked to observe how the organisms depend on each other. The expected answer—that the plants provide oxygen and the newt provides carbon dioxide—is not something the students could observe by measuring the organisms, though this is the only activity they are directed to do. Rather, it is information that was presumably supplied to them during classroom instruction or in the textbook, which they are expected to remember.

Step 6 is presented as an opportunity to draw inferences, but what the students are actually asked to do is label the living and nonliving things in the terrarium. In the "explore more" section, the students are asked to consider how an animal might use plants for food and shelter and how they might test their ideas about this. But the expected answer—that students might observe a new animal—does not engage them in thinking about how to frame a testable hypothesis or think of a way they might collect evidence to test it.

The students have 1 week to observe the terrarium and measure the organisms. They are asked to record their measurements and then to draw a diagram to show how the organisms depend on one another. However, the activity does not address what the records of the organisms' growth would reveal about how they depend on one another. Completing this set of tasks would not give students the opportunity to demonstrate an understanding of how an ecosystem functions, how to use science practices to investigate a question, how to use their observations as data for their explanations, or how to synthesize what they learned from their observations.

WHAT DO THESE EXAMPLES SHOW US?

The examples in this chapter and those that follow in subsequent chapters demonstrate a variety of approaches, but they share some common attributes. All of them require students to use science and engineering practices and crosscutting concepts while demonstrating their understanding of aspects of a disciplinary core idea. Each of them also includes multiple components: students do activities, work independently on some tasks, collaborate with their classmates, discuss their thinking, and more. In each case, the assessment gives teachers information about students' thinking and their developing understanding. But, the time students spend doing these activities is a natural part of instruction; these are not isolated assessments.

These examples illustrate some of the most important ideas that will help you adapt your own assessments:

You can use tasks with multiple components that work together to assess practices in the context of crosscutting concepts and core ideas. The tasks in "What Is Going on Inside Me?" and "Biodiversity in the Schoolyard" don't just tell you that students know key facts about the body's use of energy or biodiversity, that they can define key terms, or that they know how to create bar graphs or carry out other science practices. Instead, they show that students have engaged with the concepts, with how scientists would investigate them, and with the scientific knowledge that can help them make sense of what they observe. They have used the relevant skills for themselves to answer questions the way a scientist would. The tasks were designed to guide the students to take the multiple steps required to solve the problem.

Students engaged in active science learning do a lot of different things in the context of learning about crosscutting concepts and core ideas. New science assessments must provide information about performance expectations that describe three-dimensional learning.

It takes not only many testing sessions but also different types of tasks to capture this. In the course of the biodiversity activities, the students are outdoors observing, conferring with their classmates, entering data on an electronic device, analyzing their data, and thinking and talking about what it all means. These are things scientists do in carrying out an investigation. No single task could capture this set of interrelated tasks. Often it will make sense to have multiple tasks associated with one basic challenge, like figuring out what's going on when a body digests food.

You can use multiple assessment opportunities to collect evidence about your students' learning of complex ideas. None of these tasks by itself could provide such a detailed picture of what the students have learned. It takes time for students to demonstrate all they know and can do. They will need many—and varied—assessment opportunities over time to show what they have mastered. The writing exercise in "What Is Going on Inside Me?" only makes sense in the context of the complex activities that lead up to it, some of which can also be assessment opportunities. Similarly, the practices and the thinking that students do in the "Schoolyard" example cannot be completed in a single session. Students who successfully complete this set of four activities have shown that they can carry out an investigation and, in doing so, have learned some concepts about ecosystems and biodiversity.

Assessments can capture students' progress. Teachers—and others—are most interested in how students are progressing over time, not what they understood on a particular day. A teacher might want to know whether students grasped a concept in the course of a lesson or a unit, or if they figured out how graphing their data will help them see patterns. You know these things take time, and you want to see how students have moved forward from where they started during the course of a lesson, a unit, or a year.

The "Schoolyard" example shows how a teacher moves students gradually from learning how a task is done to demonstrating that they have mastered it. Tasks 3 and 4 target the same goal, but they have different assessment purposes. Task 3 is given midway through the biodiversity unit to provide the teacher with a sense of how far along students are and what they need to work on—as well as to give them some practice in the sort of thinking she wants them to learn. In Task 4 the students are given the opportunity to show that they have progressed in their capacity to reason and use evidence to support their thinking.

The same idea applies to thinking about what students learn in the course of a year, or across years. When assessments are designed to work together and are organized around a thoughtful description of the stages students will work through, their results will fit together to provide a rich picture of students' learning over time.

CHAPTER HIGHLIGHTS

- Assessment is an integral part of the learning experience, which would be incomplete without it. These examples show how assessments can be embedded in instruction to measure the development of three-dimensional learning over time.

- These examples are activities that would make sense for the students to do even if they were not designed to collect specific information about students' developing understanding.

- These examples show different types of tasks can be used for different types of assessment and instructional purposes.

- Assessments like these are not necessarily identified for the students as tests, and they occur at a point in instruction when the teacher needs information.

3

What Can I Learn from My Students' Work?

Changes you are making in your instruction will give you many more natural opportunities to check on your students' progress. But what can you actually learn from these opportunities? What concrete evidence can these new kinds of assessments give you about your students' thinking and what they have learned?

The examples we've looked at illustrate important elements that assessments need to have if they are to measure three-dimensional science learning. In the next two chapters we'll explore examples that show different ways to use these ideas. In this chapter we'll look at how activities that haven't traditionally been seen as assessments can be mined for valuable information. The first example, "Behavior of Air," shows how a teacher can use a class discussion as a way to assess what students understand. The second example, "Measuring Silkworms," illustrates new ways to score student work products and interpret the evidence of student learning they provide. We'll also look at some other ideas for recording assessment results and using them to support your instruction.

USING A FAMILIAR ACTIVITY AS AN ASSESSMENT

In this example designed for middle school students, sixth graders in the midst of a unit on the nature of matter are given time to discuss what they are learning. The teacher uses the discussion itself for both instructional and assessment purposes.

EXAMPLE **3** **Behavior of Air**

Level	**Middle school**
Assesses	**PRACTICES**—Developing and using models; Engaging in argument from evidence
	CROSSCUTTING CONCEPTS—Energy and matter: Flows, cycles, and conservation; Systems and system models
	DISCIPLINARY CORE IDEAS—Matter and its interactions [PS1]

This example illustrates a way to structure an activity that is part of classroom instruction almost every day— discussion—so that it can provide answers to specific questions about what students are learning. It shows how a teacher can use students' questions and misconceptions to guide the discussion.

On this day, the students are learning about a particular kind of matter: air. They draw models to explain what they observe about the behavior of air when it is pushed into a syringe. Then the teacher uses the students' discussion of the models to learn what they understand about the nature of air and what ideas need to be explored further. The discussion also supports the students in collaboratively working out answers to questions that are still not clear to them.

The activity focuses students' attention on the idea that air is made up of particles. They come to realize both that there must be empty space between moving particles and that this space allows the particles to move—either to become more densely packed or to spread apart. They develop models to explore their understanding of how a type of matter—air—behaves and to explain what they observe. Crosscutting concepts associated with energy flows and systems come into play as the students work out their explanations.

Like the two examples we saw in Chapter 2, this learning activity is embedded in a unit—in this case the assessment is not the tasks the students perform but a discussion the teacher uses to collect information about their thinking.

The teacher already knows, from earlier activities, that the students are having trouble grasping the idea that there is empty space between the molecules of air. But the students have also learned in previous lessons about several important ideas they will draw on for this activity:

- They have defined matter as anything that takes up space and has mass.

- They have concluded that gases—including air—are matter.

- They have determined through investigation that more air can be added to a container even when it already seems full and that air can be subtracted from a container—both without changing the container's size.

The students still have questions about how much more air can be forced into a space that already seems to be full. They have learned from earlier teacher-led class discussions that simply stating that the gas changes "density" does not solve the problem—it just gives it a name. They recognize that they need to figure out what actually makes it possible for differing amounts of gas (air) to expand or contract to occupy the same space. The teacher has guided them to recognize that understanding this will help them to explain what happens to any type of matter when it spreads out to occupy more space.

The students are given an empty syringe and asked to gradually pull the plunger in and out of it to explore the air pressure. They notice the pressure against their fingers when they push the plunger in and the resistance as they pull the plunger out. They find that little or no air escapes when they manipulate the plunger. They are asked to work in small groups to develop a model to explain what happens to the air so that the same amount of it can occupy the syringe regardless of the volume of space available.

The groups are asked to develop models to represent the air within the syringe in two different positions (see Figure 3-1).

This modeling activity itself is not the assessment task, though. The assessment is the class discussion in which students compare their models: it allows the teacher to diagnose the students' understanding. Figure 3-2 shows the models that five different groups of students produced to represent the air in the syringe in its first position (with the plunger partway out).

The teacher asks the class to discuss the different models with two goals in mind:

1. to explain what they observed when they manipulated the syringe, and

2. to try to reach consensus on which model best shows how air behaves.

The class has agreed that there should be "air particles" (shown in each of their models as dark dots) and that the particles are moving (shown in some models by the arrows attached to the dots).

Most of these five models represent air as a mixture of different kinds of matter, including air, odor, dust, and "other particles." What is not consistent across the models is what is represented as being *between* the particles: Models 1 and 2 show

Model 1

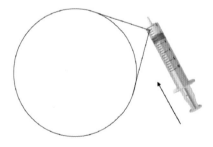

Model 2

FIGURE 3-1 Models for syringe in two positions.
SOURCE: Adapted from Krajcik et al. (2013). Reprinted with permission.

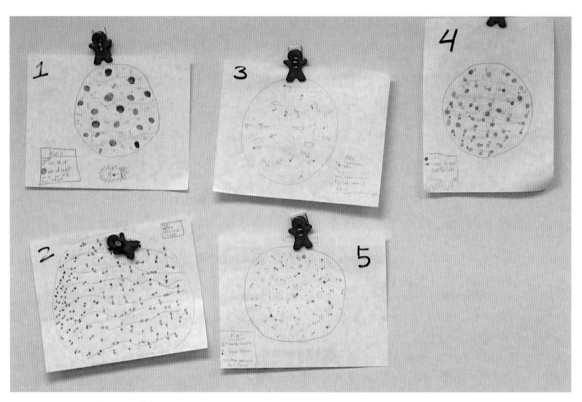

FIGURE 3-2 Student models representing air.
SOURCE: Reiser (2013). Reprinted with permission.

"wind" as the force moving the air particles; Models 3, 4, and 5 appear to show empty space between the particles.

Class Discussion as an Assessment

Exactly what, if anything, is in between the air particles emerges as a point of contention as the students discuss their models. The class agrees that the model should include air particles shown with arrows to demonstrate that the particles "are coming out in different directions," so the teacher draws several particles with arrows and asks what to put next into the model. A transcription of part of the actual classroom discussion is shown in Box 3-1.

The teacher can tell from the way the students have drawn their models that their understanding is not complete. The students have agreed that all matter, including gas, is made of particles that are moving, but many of the students do not understand what is in between these moving particles. Several students indicate that they think air is between the air particles because "air is everywhere," and some assert that the particles are all touching. Other students disagree that air can be between the particles or that air particles are touching, although they do not yet assert that there is empty space between the particles.

BOX 3-1 **STUDENT–TEACHER DIALOGUE**

Haley's objection: air is everywhere

Ms. B:	OK. Now what?
S:	Just draw like little....
Haley:	I think you should color the whole circle in, because dust ... I mean air is everywhere, so....
Miles:	The whole circle?
Ms. B:	So, I color the whole thing in.
Haley:	Yeah.
Ms. B:	So, if I do one like that, because I haven't seen one up here yet. If I color this whole thing in....
	[Ms. B colors in the whole region completely to show the air as Haley suggests.]
Michael:	Then how would you show that...?
Ms. B:	Then ask ... ask Haley some questions.
Students:	How could that be? / How would you show that?
Ms. B:	Haley, people have some questions for you.

Some students object to Haley's proposal:

Frank:	How would you show air?
Haley:	Air is everywhere, so the air would be everything.
Ss:	Yeah.
Alyssa:	But then, how would you show the other molecules? I mean, you said air is everything, but then how would you show the other...?
Ss:	Yeah, because... [multiple students talking].
Haley:	What? I didn't hear your question.
Alyssa:	Um, I said if ... You said air is everywhere, right? / Haley: Yeah. / ... so, that's why you wanted to color it in. But there's also other particles other than air, like dust and etc. and odors and things like that, so, how would you show that?
Miles:	How are we going to put in the particles?
Ms. B:	Haley, can you answer her?
Haley:	No.
Ms. B:	Why?
Haley:	I don't know. / Other student: Because there is no way.
Ms. B:	Why can't you answer? / Haley: What? / Why can't you answer?
Haley:	I don't know.
Ms. B:	Is what she's saying making sense?
Haley:	Yeah.
Ms. B:	What is it that you're thinking about?

continued

E
X
A
M
P
L
E

3

BOX 3-1 CONTINUED STUDENT–TEACHER DIALOGUE

E
X
A
M
P
L
E

3

Haley:	Um … that maybe you should take … like, erase some of it to show the odors and stuff.
Addison:	No, wait, wait!
Ms. B:	All right, call on somebody else.

Addison proposes a compromise and Ms. B pushes for clarification

Addison:	Um, I have an idea. Like since air is everywhere, you might be able to like use a different colored marker and put like, um, the other molecules in there, so you're able to show that those are in there and then air is also everywhere.
Jerome:	Yeah. I was gonna say that, or you could like erase it. If you make it all dark, you can just erase it and all of them will be.
Frank:	Just erase some parts of the, uh … yeah, yeah, just to show there's something in between it.
Ms. B:	And what's in between it?
Ss:	The dust and the particles. / Air particles. / Other odors.
Miles:	That's like the same thing over there.
Alyssa:	No, the colors are switched.
Ms. B:	Same thing over where?
Alyssa:	The big one, the consensus.
Ms. B:	On this one?
Alyssa:	Yeah.
Ms. B:	Well, what she's saying is that I should have black dots every which way, like that. [Ms. B draws the air particles touching one another in another representation, not in the consensus model, since it is Haley's idea.]
Students:	No what? / Yeah.
Ms. B:	Right?
Students:	No. / Sort of. / Yep.
Ms. B:	OK. Talk to your partners. Is this what we want? [pointing to the air particles touching one another in the diagram]

Students discuss in groups whether air particles are touching or not, and what is between the particles if anything.

SOURCE: Reiser (2013). Reprinted with permission.

Using the Results

This is an example of a formative assessment whose purpose is to help the teacher decide what instructional steps to take to support the students. The students' argument about the models plays two roles; it is an opportunity for:

- the students to defend or challenge their existing ideas, and

- the teacher to observe what the students are thinking, and to decide whether she needs to pursue the issue of what is between the particles of air.

It's also important to note that the discussion is not an accident; it was carefully structured in advance so that the teacher could gain the information she needed. In other words, the teacher does not simply bring up the issue of what is between the particles out of the blue. Rather, she uses what she has learned from the models the students created to direct the discussion. The teacher had anticipated that the empty space between particles would come up and was prepared to take advantage of that opportunity. Hearing the disagreement that emerges from the discussion helps her shape a question that will move the students forward.

The discussion gives the teacher insights into what the students were thinking that she couldn't learn from their written (and drawn) responses to a task.

Drawing the models helps the students clarify their thinking: they refine their models in response to discussion that reveals problems with them, and they use the experience of drawing and revising their models to develop increasingly clear explanations of what they have observed.

The teacher also has different kinds of evidence about what the students are thinking. She hears their discussions and questions as they develop the models. She sees their first attempts at drawing the models and hears their discussion of the differences among them. Then she sees how they revise their models based on those discussions. This combination of evidence shows the teacher how the students have used the practices of model-making and collaborative discussion of interpretations to solve their problem, as well as what they have understood about the nature of matter.

▶ The teacher wants to know exactly what students understand at a point in time so she can use the information to shape the rest of the lesson and maximize what students can learn.

▶ The assessment activity is one that would have been useful in any case, but the teacher has structured it to provide specific answers to her questions.

▶ The students need not perceive this activity as an assessment: its purpose is not summative (to grade them) but formative (to help the teacher meet their needs).

▶ This assessment is not designed to provide scorable results that might be reported beyond the classroom.

NEW WAYS TO SCORE AND EVALUATE STUDENT WORK

Using activities such as class discussions for assessment purposes requires new ways to evaluate student work. You are probably very used to learning things from class discussions and many other activities. If you want to use an activity to draw conclusions about what students know and can do, however, you'll need a structure for evaluating what your students do in response to specific tasks and determining what evidence their responses give you. You would be unlikely to score or grade a discussion, but you can structure it to help you answer very specific questions you have about your students' progress, for example.

In fact, interpretation of results is a core element of assessment, and it should be a part of the assessment design. The key to drawing valid conclusions about what your students have learned is to plan both the task and the method for scoring it based on an explicit description of what they could be expected to do in response to the task. This sort of description, in turn, should be based on clear ideas about long-term objectives—not only for the unit but also for how learning of the subject matter will develop across years.

A plan for interpreting the results—a rubric or written framework that outlines the expectations—will help you develop assessments or ways to use activities you already include in your instruction to provide assessment evidence. This rubric can also help students themselves recognize how far they have progressed and where they still have work to do. The way the students' responses are evaluated will depend on why the information is needed. As we saw with "Behavior of Air," if information is needed for formative purposes the evaluation doesn't necessarily need to be formally structured. But other kinds of assessments can be designed to provide more structured results.

You may be using a rubric that has been developed along with the assessment task, and it will help you think concretely about what kinds of information you might get from the task. If you are developing a rubric yourself, for an activity you plan to use as an assessment, the process of describing possible responses will help you think about what, exactly, you are looking for. As you start to describe the results you are seeking and how students can demonstrate the knowledge and understanding you want to measure, you may need to go back and refine the task.

"Measuring Silkworms" illustrates how a rubric serves the design of the assessment.

EXAMPLE **4** **Measuring Silkworms**

Level   **Grade 3**

Assesses   **PRACTICES**—Asking questions; Planning and carrying out investigations; Analyzing and interpreting data; Using mathematics; Constructing explanations; Engaging in argument from evidence; Communicating information

CROSSCUTTING CONCEPTS—Patterns

DISCIPLINARY CORE IDEAS—Structure and function: Organisms have macroscopic structures that allow for growth [LS1.A]; Growth and development of organisms: Organisms have unique and diverse life cycles [LS1.B]

This example illustrates how an assessment that is carefully designed together with its scoring rubric can help a teacher gain deep insights into students' understanding. Sample student responses are used in the rubric.

Third graders do this activity as part of a unit on the growth of silkworm larvae. The interactive activity is both an opportunity for the students to learn about the distinction between an individual organism's growth and growth patterns across a population and an opportunity for their teacher to assess their learning.

As the class period begins, the students have already been working with the silkworms and identified some questions they want to answer. On this day, they measure the silkworm larvae and record the data. The teacher asks the students to think of ways they might display the measurements they have taken that will communicate what they are noticing about the larval growth that day. What is assessed is the way the students decide to display their data: their choices about this tell the teacher what they have understood about how to use techniques for displaying data to interpret what they have observed. The teacher supports the students in developing the kinds of thinking the activity is designed to teach about data display.

The teacher has some guidance in what to expect from the students: the researchers and teachers who designed this unit provided descriptions of six levels of performance that might be expected from third-grade students (shown in Table 3-1). This kind of table is one way to structure a scoring rubric: for each level there is a clear description of what students demonstrate they can do, along with an example or two illustrating what that level response looks like for third-grade students. Researchers who develop assessments like this test them on groups of students and use what they learn to refine the tasks and the rubrics. They can also collect responses that are good examples of each of the six levels. You can do the same thing. If you work with your colleagues you can, over time, build a collection of sample student work and refine the way you design your rubrics.

The process of describing possible responses will help you think about what, exactly, you are looking for.

Figure 3-3 shows one example of how a group of third-grade students decided to display their data (it has been redrawn for clarity). This group of students ordered by magnitude each of the 261 measurements they took. As a result, their display occupied 5 feet of wall space in the classroom! One can see the range of the data at a glance in their display, but the icons they use to represent each millimeter of length are not uniform. These students are at Level 2.

Another group of students used equal-sized intervals to show equivalence among classes of lengths (see Figure 3-4). By counting the number of cases within each interval, the students made a center clump visible. This display makes the *shape* of the data more visible. The use of space was not uniform, however, and that produces misleading impressions of the frequency with which longer or shorter larvae occur. These students are at Level 3.

The third display shows how some students used the measurement scale and counts of cases. Because of the difficulties they experienced with arranging the display on paper, they reduced the size for all counts greater than 6 (see Figure 3-5). These students are at Level 4.

TABLE 3-1 Performance Levels for "Measuring Silkworms" Activity

Level	Performance	What the Students Do/Examples
1	Create or interpret displays without reference to the goals of the inquiry.	"We grouped even and odd numbers because we like even and odd numbers." "I put these two values (19 and 11) on the top because that's my birthday—November 19!" "This display has lots of numbers."
2	Interpret data displays as collections of individual cases: Construct/interpret data by considering ordinal properties.	"The data start out with the lowest measurement and go to the highest one." Student creates display by ordering data as a list or case-value graph.
	Interpret data displays as collections of individual cases: Concentrate on specific data points without relating them to any structure in the data.	Student identifies maximum and minimum values. "The only thing I can tell is this (193) is the highest." "154 is the number in the middle of the list (without ordering the data)." "This number is the biggest."
3	Notice or construct groups of similar values.	Student creates unordered bins and comments on, e.g., the number of occurrences of 40s versus the number of 50s. When asked to name bins in a preset display, assigns discontinuous and/or unequal intervals, such as 2–25, 26–36, 37–45. Creates equal interval bins but leaves out intermediate intervals. Notices "plateaus" in the display or in a group of similar values. "This number, 193, is really different because the others are all between 160 and 165."
4	Recognize in, or apply scale properties to, the data: Recognize the effects of changing bin size on the shape of the distribution.	"If we make the bin size wider, the tower in the center will pop up."
	Recognize in, or apply scale properties to, the data: Display data in ways that use continuous scale (when appropriate) to see holes and clumps in the data.	Uses number line or bar type graph to show proportions.
5	Quantify aggregate property of the display using one or more of the following: ratio, proportion, or percent.	"I found out that measurements between 45 and 55 were 70 percent of our measurements. So, I guess the true height is somewhere between 45 and 55."
	Recognize that a display provides information about the data as a collective (set).	Students annotate their displays to show percentages within particular regions. "When we measure different things we keep getting a bell shape. That's because we tend to get around the real measure most of the time but sometimes we make big mistakes."
6	Discuss how general patterns or trends are either exemplified by or missing from subsets of cases.	Relate qualities of the case in the activity as an example of the general qualities of a region of data. Notice that the subset of cases does not seem to fit the trends observed or conjectured.

NOTE: "Bins" refers to categories of data points.
SOURCE: Adapted from Wilson et al. (2013).

EXAMPLE

4

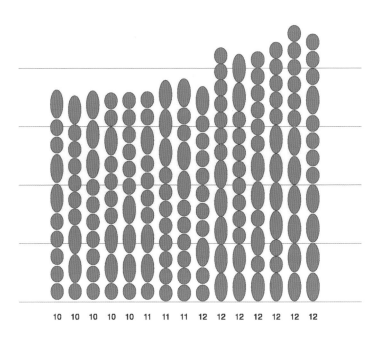

10 10 10 10 10 11 11 11 12 12 12 12 12 12 12

FIGURE 3-3 Facsimile of student representation of silkworm larvae growth.
SOURCE: Lehrer (2011). Reprinted with permission.

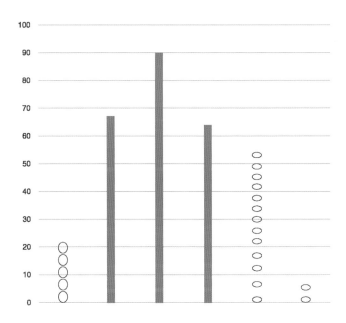

FIGURE 3-4 Facsimile of student-invented representation of groups of data values for silkworm larvae growth.
NOTE: The original used icons to represent the organisms in each interval.
SOURCE: Lehrer (2011). Reprinted with permission.

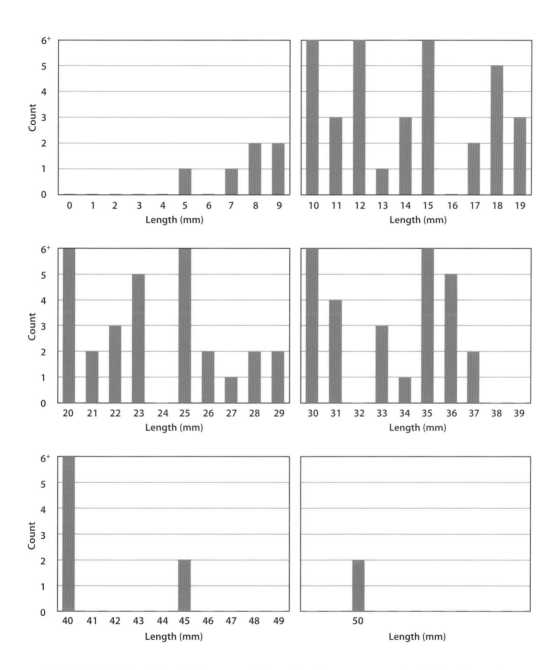

FIGURE 3-5 Student-invented representation using the measurement scale for silkworm larvae growth.

SOURCE: Lehrer (2011). Reprinted with permission.

Using the Results

This assessment can be adapted for both formative and summative purposes. The teacher might use this activity in the midst of instruction to see what students understand about how different ways of representing their data emphasize or convey different information. She can use the results to follow up on areas the students did not fully understand. In this case, to help students develop their competence at representing data, the teacher then invites them to talk about what each of the different ways of displaying the data show and do not show. Through this discussion the teacher focuses the students on the idea that all representational choices emphasize certain features of data and obscure others. During this conversation, the students are guided to think about how space is used in the displays and to appreciate the basis for some of the conventions people use to display data.

The teacher also guides the conversation to some mathematical points related to the display of data: the use of order, counting, and interval and measurement scale to create different shapes in representing data. This teacher-led discussion helps the students discern the bell-like shape that is often characteristic of natural variation.

The focus on the shape of the data is a gentle introduction to the idea of variability. The teacher uses that to get the students thinking about larval growth. For example, as some students examined Figure 3-5, they noticed that the tails of the distribution were comparatively sparse, especially for the longer silkworm larvae, and they wondered why. They speculated that this shape suggested that the organisms did not all have equal access to resources. They related this possibility to differences in the timing of larval hatching and guessed that larvae that hatched earlier might have begun eating and growing sooner and therefore acquired an advantage in the competition for food.

The idea that competition helps to account for the variability and growth the students observed is a new kind of explanation for them. This idea helps them begin to think beyond individual organisms and consider what is happening to the whole population of silkworms.

This activity could also be used for a summative purpose, after students have had more experience with the core ideas in this unit and practice with ways of structuring data displays and thinking and talking about what they show. The levels in the map in Table 3-1 describe the types of reasoning third-grade students are likely to show as they consider possible ways to display their data. The descriptions of the performance levels provide a way to interpret the significance of these differences. The researchers who developed this map based it in part on the results of similar activities, in which elementary students worked with data and statistics to develop similar descriptions of performance levels that apply more broadly—beyond this activity.

Because these levels were developed in advance, based on instructional goals and information about what third-grade students can be expected to do, it would be reasonable to compare results for different groups of students given the same task, for example, or to use the activity at the end of a unit to see whether students had met performance expectations. As researchers and practitioners continue to collect student work and develop descriptions of learning progressions, there will be more resources to draw on. By collaborating with your colleagues in developing descriptions of performance levels and reviewing the kinds of responses your students come up with, you can refine and improve your "maps" of what your students can do.

Using Example Student Responses

Examples of student work are useful for illustrating what different levels of performance look like. Using them in the interpretation of results from new types of assessments provides a way to make descriptions of a learning progression concrete. The scoring rubric in Table 3-2 was developed for a task that assessed students' understanding of the core ideas that species develop new traits because of random genetic processes (e.g., mutations) and that the new traits might be either helpful or harmful or have no effect on survival. The most important point in the instruction was that the genetic processes and the new traits that result are random. The traits become more common if they benefit the species; therefore, organisms that have the trait are more likely to successfully reproduce.

The levels described here correspond to a map that researchers had developed showing how student understanding of these ideas may move from an everyday understanding to a scientifically accurate understanding. This rubric does not assign numeric levels, but it does describe responses that demonstrate increasing levels of understanding, with "trait not present" describing the most minimal response.

A scoring guide like this helps the teacher use the students' responses to see which students have reached the highest level—or upper anchor of performance—and understand the main idea about random mutation. Other students will demonstrate that they have heard some of the terms without developing an integrated understanding of the way this process works. Still others have incorrect ideas—

TABLE 3-2 Rubric for Assessment of Genetic Processes

Level	Description	Example Student Response
Random mutations	Student describes one or more of the random genetic mechanisms by which new traits arise.	A species changes over time because of random mutations and gene shuffling. Random mutations can cause a change in a species' gene pool. And gene shuffling is different combinations of genes that come from the parents. If species are separated long enough, the species' gene pool changes.
Environment causes change with genetic basis	Changes occur as a result of genetic mutations in direct response to the environment and/or not random.	Animals mutate to fit in with their natural surroundings. So becoming darker helps to keep them in camouflage.
Unclear or vague	Student refers to mutations or random changes leading to new traits but does not describe a mechanism for how that happens.	If a mutation happens it can [affect] the whole species by creating a variety of differences, from color change to more or less help against gathering food and protecting against predators.
Trait not present	Description of differences in traits not given at genetic level or denial of change in genes.	I picked my answer because none of the [others] seemed all the way correct.

SOURCE: Furtak and Heredia (2014, p. 1004). Reprinted with permission from John Wiley & Sons, Inc.

such as the idea that organisms can intentionally develop traits that will be beneficial in their environments.

The second example (see Table 3-3) is from a unit for sixth graders on the solar system and the relationship between the Sun and Earth's seasons. The unit engages the students in the practices of discourse, developing an argument from evidence, and modeling as they explore the crosscutting concept of energy and the core ideas about Earth and the solar system. A set of five descriptions of the increasingly sophisticated understanding that can be expected of sixth-grade students is the scoring guide, or learning progression, for this assessment.

At the start of the unit, the teacher recognizes that many of the students have made observations about the seasons that she will want to address, such as that fluctuations in Earth's distance from the Sun are the cause of changes in the seasons and that the shape of Earth's orbit around the Sun is an oval rather than very nearly circular. The teacher gives the students a model of Earth and a lightbulb to represent the Sun and encourages them to explore what happens to the lengths and intensity of sunlight at different locations in the Northern and Southern hemispheres as Earth follows its orbit and tilts toward the star Polaris.

TABLE 3-3 Learning Progressions for Assessment of Seasons

Level	Sophistication of Understanding	Example Student Descriptions of Phenomena
5 upper anchor	Students understand that seasons on Earth and changes in temperature are caused by angle and intensity of sunlight and length of day.	"In North America in June, the Sun is higher in the sky causing longer daylight hours and more direct rays from the Sun." "Earth's North Pole always points toward Polaris and in June Earth is tilted so the Northern Hemisphere is getting more direct sunlight."
4	Students recognize that Earth's tilt on its axis changes the length of day but may not be able to apply this understanding to temperature or the crosscutting concept of energy.	"Because Earth is facing the Sun it receives more sunlight and gets warmer." "Temperatures at the equator are warm because the equator has summer all year."
3	Students may have naïve understanding of the seasons.	"The Sun is farther away from Earth in winter and closer in summer." "The [Sun] gives off more heat in the summer."
2	Students are aware that shadows [from] the Sun have different lengths and that length of days changes throughout the year.	"As the day gets longer, so does my shadow from the Sun." "In the summer, the days are longer than they are in the winter."
1 lower anchor	Students notice a change in the times the Sun rises and sets during the year.	"The Sun rises early in the morning in summer." "It gets dark earlier in the winter."

SOURCE: Huff and Duschl (2016). Reprinted with permission.

Table 3-3 lays out the range of expected responses using precise descriptions of each level, together with sample responses, to illustrate what each can look like.

Collecting these sorts of details about the students' reasoning allows the teacher to address the understanding students demonstrate between the lower and upper anchors in the performance expectations for the unit. He could respond very precisely to the areas where they are struggling by:

- using the students' own descriptions of the phenomena in his instruction, and

- focusing instruction on evidence that could be used to help students examine and modify their ideas.

WHAT DO THESE EXAMPLES SHOW US?

"Behavior of Air" shows how a classroom discussion can be used to assess three-dimensional understanding. The activity is structured to focus the students' attention on particular ideas about matter and to guide them on how to use the modeling activity to explore their thinking. The teacher uses the discussion of the students' models of air particles to identify what they don't understand and then to support them in collaborating to resolve the differences their models reveal. This task assesses both their understanding of the concept and their proficiency with the practices of modeling and developing oral arguments about what they have observed.

This is a formative assessment designed to help the teacher and the students in real time. With formative assessments there usually is no need to assign scores to individual students. Instead of scoring rubrics, you might use more informal criteria that will help you quickly see what you need to know in order to make instructional decisions and better support your students. In this example, the curriculum designer used information about the challenges students are likely to have (this is often information a learning progression can provide) to develop questions and prompts for guiding the discussion.

"Measuring Silkworms" illustrates the use of a different set of three-dimensional activities for both formative and summative purposes. In the course of doing these activities, students learn about how data displays can convey ideas; they also learn about why professional scientists have developed certain conventions for doing this. They likewise learn how such mathematical practices as ordering and counting data influence the shapes the data displays take. The activities work interactively: as the students learn a practice (data representation as an aspect of data analysis), they also learn about a crosscutting concept (recognizing and interpreting patterns) and a core idea (variation in a population).

Creating the displays is a learning activity for the students, but it is also a formative assessment, a source of evidence for their teacher about what they are learning. The performance levels could be used formatively or summatively. The rubrics for the assessment of genetic processes and understanding the seasons (see Tables 3-2 and 3-3) illustrate how sample student responses can be used to make the descriptions in a rubric more concrete.

What these examples have in common is that they allow the teacher to group the students into categories, which helps with the difficult task of making sense of many kinds of student thinking. They also provide tools for helping the teacher decide what to do next or for assigning scores to individual students.

CHAPTER HIGHLIGHTS

- A critical task in adapting science activities for use as either formative or summative assessments is to develop a clear description of what will be assessed by each task—what students will demonstrate. This description will begin with the specific performance expectations you want to measure. You can use that, together with examples of students' responses to the task, to develop a scoring rubric.

- To use an informal activity such as a class discussion or a collaborative data modeling exercise as an assessment, you need to structure it ahead of time, based on what you know about the misunderstandings students are likely to have and the specific goals you want the students to accomplish. You can use planned questions and strategies to redirect the students and focus their attention on the concepts you are assessing.

- You can also use your expectations for student learning to develop a structure for interpreting the information you get from the assessment. This might be an informal checklist you have for making sure the students have understood what they need to know in order to move forward, or it might be a more formal rubric for scoring their performance.

4

Building New Kinds of Assessments into the Flow of Your Instruction

The 2012 framework and the Next Generation Science Standards (NGSS) have been described as "transforming"[1] science education because they call for substantial changes not only in science instruction but also in what happens at the school, district, and state levels. Changes in instruction, curriculum, textbooks and other materials, and assessments are already taking place. But each district and state is approaching these changes at its own pace and in its own way, and changes in large-scale assessment will likely come after other changes (see Box 4-1). Your own district and state may not have new standards that reflect the framework, or they may not be far along in adapting new assessments. As a result, your students may still need to take traditional large-scale science assessments.

Regardless of the pace of change in your school, district, and state—or of how quickly district or state tests change—adapting your assessments will be a critical aspect of adapting your instructional approach to engage your students in doing science for themselves and learning in a three-dimensional way. You can begin using new kinds of assessment results right away.

The better your assessments are at engaging all students and helping you see what they understand and where they need more support, the fairer they are. Approaches to assessment that use a range of formats and provide students with many opportunities to demonstrate what they know and can do can give you insights that will help you meet the needs of students from diverse cultural and language backgrounds. They will also help you make sure all your students have a meaningful opportunity to learn.

In this chapter we explore how you can use the ideas from earlier chapters to adapt the assessments you already use and to design new ones. We'll look at

---

[1]See http://www.livescience.com/40283-ngss-science-standards-change-education.html [April 2016].

BOX 4-1 DISTRICTS AND STATES ADAPTING

Each state has its own approach to changes such as adopting new standards and adapting assessments. The *Guide to Implementing the Next Generation Science Standards* provides a thorough overview of what is involved and it emphasizes that this will have to be a gradual process (http://www.nap.edu/catalog/18802 [May 2016]). California and Maryland are two states that have the process under way and illustrate different ways to proceed with the implementation of the Next Generation Science Standards (NGSS).

California adopted the NGSS in 2013. The state's process for implementing the standards began with rewriting its curriculum framework and evaluation criteria and developing a detailed implementation plan. The plan included a process for integrating the new science standards with the Common Core State Standards for English/Language Arts and Mathematics, which it adopted in 2010. The State Board of Education voted in March 2016 to proceed with a proposed design for a summative assessment program that will align with the new standards, and it expects to begin administering these assessments in the 2018–2019 school year.

See http://www.cde.ca.gov/pd/ca/sc/documents/scienceimplementationplan120214.pdf [September 2016] for more information about the implementation plan.

Maryland mapped out a five-phase plan for implementing the NGSS:

Phase 1, 2012–2014: Exploration, awareness, and statewide capacity building

Phase 2, 2014–2015: Classroom transitions, shifts, and practices

Phase 3, 2015–2016: Leveraging materials, resources, and expertise

Phase 4, 2016–2017: Statewide application, assessment, and coordination

Phase 5, 2017–2018: Full pre-K–12 implementation.*

See http://mdk12.msde.maryland.gov/share/VSC/NGSS_IPD0.pdf [August 2016] for information about the process.

See http://mdk12.msde.maryland.gov/instruction/curriculum/Science/index.html [August 2016] for the Maryland science standards.

*Maryland may delay development of pre-K standards.

some examples that illustrate more options for collecting evidence about your students' learning and for using assessment results in the flow of your instruction. We'll also explore possibilities for using your current resources in new ways.

APPLYING NEW APPROACHES

As you develop lessons, you probably already think about when you will assess what your students have learned. Taking that idea a step further means thinking even more specifically about what types of information it would be helpful to have at each stage of an instructional unit and designing the activities your students will be doing so they can be a source for that information. The examples in this chapter illustrate more ways to use the ideas we discussed in Chapters 2 and 3.

We saw with the "Biodiversity in the Schoolyard" example (see Chapter 2) that the same task could be adapted for different purposes at different stages in an instructional unit. A task may first be used for formative purposes, with supports that help shape the experience for the students and help the teacher see what they may need help with (e.g., as in Task 3). Later, a very similar task is used for a summative purpose, without the supports, so the teacher can use the results to grade the students' work (e.g., as in Task 4). Adapting an activity that is an important part of a unit so you can also use it to collect evidence about your students' learning is a key tool of the new approach. The first example we will explore in this chapter, "Climate Change," is another example that shows how a task can be customized.

We have seen how a seemingly simple assessment task can provide a lot of information if it is carefully designed. In the "What Is Going on Inside Me?" example (see Chapter 2), the students do a writing exercise not unlike many others. It gets its power, however, from the way it fits into a sequence of activities and from the clear expectations of what students can weave together at this stage of the unit. Similarly, in the "Behavior of Air" example (see Chapter 3), the teacher has reason to expect the students will have a range of understanding and is prepared to use a classroom discussion—a familiar activity—for very specific (formative) purposes. In "Movement of Water," the second example we explore in this chapter, the teacher also uses this kind of planning to collect evidence from a class discussion for formative purposes.

Level	**High school**
Assesses	**PRACTICES**—Analyzing and interpreting data; Using a model to predict phenomena
	CROSSCUTTING CONCEPTS—Systems and system models
	DISCIPLINARY CORE IDEAS—Ecosystems: Interactions, energy, and dynamics [LS2]; Earth and human activity [ESS3-5]

This example—like "What Is Going on Inside Me?" in Chapter 2—illustrates a way to adapt a task so that it can be used for instruction and then, later, to assess learning. It uses computer software that makes it possible to enhance the activity in interesting ways, but the ideas could be applied without this technology.

This task is part of a computer-based climate change curriculum for high school students. The software allows teachers to tailor how they use the task depending on what they would like to assess and the stage of learning their students have reached. Using the software, the teachers select what degree of supporting information and guidance the program will offer their students. Note, however, that this kind of customizing could also be done without the software.

The task engages students in using geoscience data and the results from global climate models to support predictions about the effect climate change will have on particular organisms and ecosystems. It assesses their understanding of the impacts of climate change on organisms and ecosystems and crosscutting concepts about systems and system, along with their facility at analyzing and interpreting data and using modeling to explore possible outcomes.

Teachers use this task at the end of the unit, at which point the students have selected a focal species (i.e., one of the native species within a particular ecosystem they would like to study) and have learned about its needs and how it is distributed in the ecosystem. They will also have learned about a set of model-based climate projections, called Future 1, 2, and 3, that represent more and less severe climate change effects. (These are shown in Figure 4-1.[2]) In the lessons leading up to this assessment task, the students were guided to make and justify predictions about their focal species.

The goal of the assessment task is to provide teachers and students with evidence on the question "How will climate change affect my focal species?" In a previous activity, students made and tested predictions about

---

[2]The projections are taken from the Intergovernmental Panel on Climate Change (IPCC) data predictions for the year 2100 (Intergovernmental Panel on Climate Change, 2007).

	Population growth rate	Energy use per person	Proportion clean energy	Total CO_2 emissions by 2100 (gigatons)
Future 1	Fast	Low	Low	1,862
Future 2	Slow	High	High	1,499
Future 3	Slow	Low	High	983

FIGURE 4-1 Three simplified future scenarios for the year 2100.
NOTE: CO_2 = carbon dioxide.
SOURCE: Adapted from Peters et al. (2012).

whether their focal species could live in a particular area. Now they are asked to predict the future distributions of their focal species under various climate scenarios.

When students begin the task, the program presents them with the materials that they will need to make and support a prediction in answer to the question, "In Future 3, would climate change impact your focal species?" (Again, the program makes this more convenient but it could be done without that.)

All students are given:

- Information about the three different climate change scenarios (see Figure 4-1) and

- a map of North America that illustrates the current and the predicted distribution of locations of optimal biotic and abiotic[3] conditions for the red squirrel, as predicted by the Future 3 scenario (see Figure 4-2).

The program asks the students to provide:

- a claim (the prediction) as to whether or not they believe the information about the three scenarios suggests that climate change will affect their chosen animal;

- reasoning that connects their prediction to the model-based evidence, such as noting that their species needs a particular prey to survive; and

- evidence from the models—drawn from the information in the maps of model-based climate projections. For example, students might indicate whether or not the distribution of conditions needed by the animal and its food source in the future scenario will be significantly different from what it is at present.

---

[3]The biotic component of an environment consists of the living species that populate it, while the abiotic components are the nonliving influences such as geography, soil, water, and climate that are specific to the particular region.

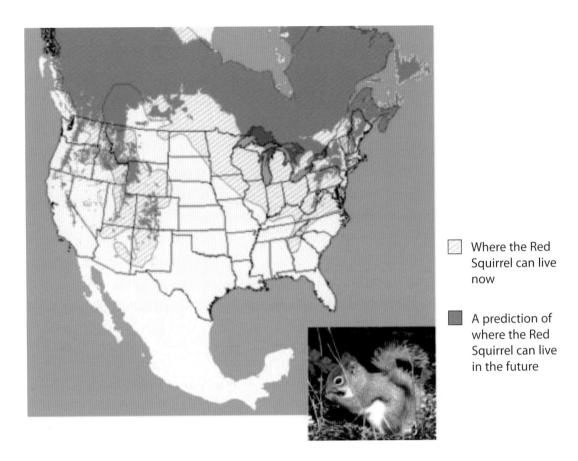

Where the Red
Squirrel can live
now

A prediction of
where the Red
Squirrel can live
in the future

FIGURE 4-2 Current and predicted Future 3 distribution for the red squirrel.
SOURCE: Songer et al. (2013). Reprinted with permission.

If the teacher is using this task for instruction and/or to assess where students are, she can opt to give the students access to a tutorial that teaches about how to develop predictions. This feature of the program prompts students as to what is needed and records their responses in a database that teachers and students can use.

The teacher can choose whether or not to allow students access to the pop-up text that describes what is meant by a claim or by evidence. If the students have already spent time learning about how to make and support a claim, the teacher can choose not to give them access to these supports and use their responses to develop unit or course grades, for example.

Table 4-1 shows the rubric used to code student responses to the question "Will climate change affect where the red squirrel can live in the future?" Table 4-2 shows five sample student responses. Teachers can use this display to quickly assess the range of responses in their class and make decisions about future instruction based on those responses.

TABLE 4-1 Scoring Rubric for Red Squirrel Prediction

Level 5

Demonstration of a complete knowledge product that effectively incorporates relevant scientific terminology.
Elaboration:
Appropriate DCI and CC are used in the explanation/prediction, which are detailed/elaborated. The explanation/prediction includes a claim supported by relevant evidence along with appropriate reasoning that links the claim and evidence.
AND
the product effectively incorporates relevant scientific terminology.

Level 4

Demonstration of a complete knowledge product but lacking effective incorporation of relevant scientific terminology.
Elaboration:
Appropriate DCI and CC are used in the explanation/prediction, which are detailed/elaborated. The explanation/prediction includes a claim supported by relevant evidence along with appropriate reasoning that links the claim and evidence.
AND
the product does not incorporate any relevant scientific terminology, or uses only some of the relevant scientific terminology.

Level 3

Demonstration of a partially complete knowledge product that is appropriately elaborated upon and effectively incorporates some relevant scientific terminology.
Elaboration:
Appropriate DCI and/or CC are used in the explanation/prediction, which are detailed/elaborated. The explanation/prediction is partially complete as one of the three parts of the explanation (claim, reasoning, evidence) is missing or not explicitly stated.
AND
the product effectively incorporates some relevant scientific terminology.

Level 2

Demonstration of a partially complete knowledge product that lacks elaboration and does not incorporate relevant scientific terminology.
Elaboration:
Appropriate DCI and/or CC are used in the explanation/prediction, which are not adequately detailed/elaborated. The explanation/prediction is partially complete as two of the three parts of the explanation (claim, reasoning, evidence) are missing or not explicitly stated.
AND
the product does not effectively incorporate relevant scientific terminology.

Level 1

Demonstration of an incomplete knowledge product that lacks elaboration and does not incorporate relevant scientific terminology.
Elaboration:
Only uses appropriate DCI, which is not adequately detailed/elaborated.
AND
the product does not effectively incorporate relevant scientific terminology.

Level 0

Demonstration of an inaccurate knowledge product.
Elaboration:
Inappropriate DCI or scientifically inaccurate use of the DCI.

NOTE: CC = crosscutting concept; DCI = disciplinary core idea.
SOURCE: Songer et al. (2013). Reprinted with permission.

TABLE 4-2 Sample Student Responses

Level	Response	Characteristics of Response
0	No, because the red squirrel lives in hot and cold areas so if the temperature rises, the red squirrel could still live in warm areas so I don't think climate change.	• Based on information provided, the response is scientifically inaccurate.
1	Yes, because the temperature can be too hot or too cold for it.	• Accurate claim. • Claim is supported by a conjecture. • Response lacks elaboration. • Absence of scientific terminology.
2	Yes, the red squirrel will have to move because of climate change. They will have to move farther north because they will not like it where they are found now.	• Accurate claim supported by evidence. • Source of evidence is not explicitly stated. • Incomplete reasoning to link the claim and evidence (e.g., "they will not like it"). • Response lacks elaboration. • Absence of scientific terminology.
3	Yes, climate change will affect the red squirrels in the future. The red squirrel will have to migrate North mostly into Canada because it will be hot in America. This is shown in the map in the purple color.	• Accurate claim supported by evidence. • Source of evidence is explicitly stated. • Incomplete reasoning to link the claim and evidence (e.g., "because it will be hot in America"). • Response is detailed/elaborate (e.g., claim is a complete sentence answering the question; evidence as well as its source is described). • Use of some scientific terminology correctly ("migrate").
4	Yes, it will. In the map you can see that the area where the red squirrel can live in the future is in the North where the climate is colder. If the amount of carbon dioxide in the air increases, so will the temperature. If the temperature rises where the red squirrel may live, that place might not have suitable habitat for it anymore.	• Accurate claim supported by evidence, and reasoning links claim and evidence. • Source of evidence is explicitly stated. • Response is detailed/elaborate (e.g., reasoning described in detail). • Presence of some scientific terminology used accurately ("habitat").
5	Yes, climate change will affect where the red squirrel can live. Scientists are predicting that the red squirrel will have to move north because if CO_2 emissions increase, there will be more carbon dioxide in the atmosphere and the greenhouse effect will cause the temperatures to rise. This will force the squirrel to migrate to regions where the temperature is cool enough for it to survive and get the food that it needs. This is what we can see in the map where the future areas have moved up to Canada.	• Accurate claim supported by evidence, and reasoning links claim and evidence. • Source of evidence is explicitly stated. • Response is detailed/elaborate. • Presence of scientific terminology ("scientists are predicting," "migrate," "CO_2 emissions," "greenhouse effect") used accurately.

SOURCE: Songer et al. (2013). Reprinted with permission.

E
X
A
M
P
L
E

5

Presenting this task using interactive computer technology has several advantages. It makes it possible to conveniently present data from several sources to the students. The software also makes summary information about the quality and range of student responses continuously available to teachers, who can then adapt their instruction to quickly address students' misunderstandings or gaps in understanding. The software also makes it easy to customize the support and resources the students have access to.

The computer models make these tasks easier for a teacher to use, but the most important aspects of these tasks can be done without them. Like other tasks we've looked at, these assessment tasks provide students with information they can use to construct evidence-based explanations or predictions about the phenomenon, even if the data are not provided on a computer and it is not possible to work with it interactively.

These assessment tasks provide students with information they can use to construct evidence-based explanations or predictions about the phenomenon.

With both this and the "Diversity in the Schoolyard" example from Chapter 2, it is easy to see how a particular task structure can be used for multiple purposes: to instruct, to check student progress and see what supports are needed, or to make summative judgments about what students have learned. The tasks vary in terms of what the students have access to as they work through them and how much guidance they are receiving. The teacher adapts the prompts her students receive about the characteristics of a scientific explanation, where to look for evidence, how to approach a task, or when they have taken a wrong turn. These variations in the task are based on students' proficiency levels and the teacher's expectations about what students can accomplish without assistance. The teacher uses these results both to shape instruction to help students with areas that are difficult as well as to collect summative evidence at the end of the unit.

EXAMPLE **6** **Movement of Water**

Level   **Middle school**

Assesses   **PRACTICES**—Modeling, constructing examples

              CROSSCUTTING CONCEPTS—Systems and system models

              DISCIPLINARY CORE IDEAS—The roles of water in Earth's surface processes [ESS2.C]

In this example the teacher uses a simple technology to assess students' understanding while a discussion is going on and then uses the results to modify her next steps to address areas students need to work on.

In this example, the students work through an activity and then talk about it in a way that seems like a natural next step in the unit. In this case, though, the teacher has deliberately prepared for the discussion so that she can use it to collect information about their learning. The task is a class discussion that is used for formative assessment purposes as part of a middle school curriculum on Earth Systems. In the course of the unit, students have investigated weathering, erosion, and deposition, and they are learning about:

- a *core disciplinary idea*: how the properties and movement of water shape Earth's surface and affect its systems;

- a *crosscutting concept*: systems and system models (models of geosphere-hydrosphere interactions); and

- the *practice* of developing an explanation based on evidence.

Before the day of this discussion, the students have already built physical models of water flowing through a landscape using stream tables (models of stream flows set up in large boxes filled with sedimentary material and tilted so that water can flow through). They have developed predictions about how water will move sediment and how that process affects the deposition of surface and subsurface materials.

At this point in the unit, the teacher wants to help students make sense of what they have learned and to check their understanding of the process of deposition. She uses a projection screen to show the students the two photographs in Figure 4-3.

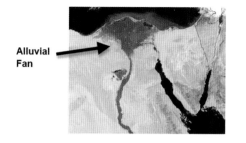

FIGURE 4-3 Illustrations for multiple-choice question.
SOURCES: NASA/GSFC/JPL/LaRC, MISR Science Team (2013) and Los Angeles County Museum of Art (2013).

E
X
A
M
P
L
E

6

She then presents multiple-choice questions for the students to answer using their clickers, such as this one:

The green areas marked above show the place where a river flows into an ocean. Why does this river look like a triangle (or fan) where it flows into the ocean? Be prepared to explain your response.

A. Sediment is settling there as the land becomes flatter.
B. The water can flow all over the place just before it meets the ocean.
C. The river is transporting sediment to the ocean.
D. Finer sediments suspended in the water are being deposited there.

The teacher uses clicker technology to collect individual student responses to the questions. This technology (also known as a classroom response system) allows students to use handheld clickers to respond to questions. The responses are gathered by a central receiver and immediately tallied for the teacher—or the whole class—to see. The teacher then uses these responses to decide what students need next. For example, she might set up small-group discussions that address misunderstandings, give certain students supplementary activities, or address a widely shared misunderstanding with the whole group.

This is a fairly straightforward activity—one that could be done without the technology (although the teacher would not have automatically generated tallies of the results). For example, students could raise their hands to signal which answer they choose, or they could mark their selection on a slip of paper. Either way, the teacher can prepare in advance to use this simple activity in a very targeted way.

In this case, the questions have been tested in classrooms so the response choices offered reflect common student misunderstandings. The students' responses give the teacher information about what proportion of the class holds any of these common misunderstandings; the teacher also sees how individual students respond. If you develop a similar assessment, you and your colleagues can collect evidence about areas students struggle with and build that knowledge into the design of the task and the questions you use in the discussion.

Working in pairs or small groups, students discuss the reasoning that led them to their answers. The teacher helps get each group started by asking them to think about why someone might select each of the options, implying that any of them could be a reasonable response. The whole class reconvenes and the groups offer explanations for their choices to the whole class. The teacher encourages students to compare their own reasoning to that of others (the unit provides suggested discussion strategies). Then the students vote again, using their clickers.

Rather than highlighting who got the questions right and who got them wrong or placing students into ability groups, you are using the evidence you've collected about the class as a whole to structure a responsive lesson.

The responses help the teacher see which students are still having difficulties. The program includes a set of "contingent activities" teachers can use to improve the students' understanding. Each of these contingent activities focuses on a particular learning objective, such as interpreting models, constructing explanations, or making predictions. So, for example, students who are having difficulty with the sample question might work independently on an activity in which they watch an animation of deposition and then make a prediction about a pattern they might expect to find at the mouth of a river where sediment is being deposited.

An activity like this can allow you to use your students' responses to strategic questions to get them engaged in a back and forth about the possible answers and naïve conceptions. Rather than highlighting who got the questions right and who got them wrong or placing students into ability groups, you are using the evidence you've collected about the class as a whole to structure a responsive lesson.

Instructional activities can be adapted for different assessment purposes. A learning activity might be used to collect specific information about students' progress—which the teacher uses to shape instruction. With changes, such as limiting the resources and supports students have access to, it could later be used to collect evidence of how well students have mastered learning goals.

TAKING ADVANTAGE OF TECHNOLOGY

"Movement of Water" uses clicker technology that allows students to register their responses to multiple-choice questions instantly, and it likewise allows the teacher to see tallies of those responses immediately. Even if you don't have clicker technology, however, collecting fast responses to questions that are planned ahead of time to reflect common misconceptions can help you identify students who need more time with a concept or activity, or it can give you a sense of how to structure small-group discussions. For example, you might tally your students' responses on a white board if you don't have clicker technology. The same idea holds for other technologies as well. You may have access to sophisticated technology—or you may be able to take ideas from it that you can use in other ways to collect information without purchasing expensive software.

New technologically advanced tools, specifically designed to support instruction and assessment, are available every year, and they have a lot to offer. Sophisticated technology may make it possible to measure types of learning that are very difficult to measure in other ways. Computer simulations can give students access to digital versions of experiences that would otherwise be out of reach: for instance, experiments that involve expensive or dangerous materials or specialized equipment, or ones that would need to be carried out in particular settings or conditions not available in a school setting. They can allow students to carry out lengthy investigations in a compressed time frame. This is a capability that may be worth an investment because it allows students to engage in practices that wouldn't be possible without it.

Other technology can make it easier to collect, record, and analyze data. Technology can make it possible for students to respond to assessment tasks in different ways that may be as easy to score as multiple-choice tasks but provide more information. For example, students might be able to indicate how they would classify something by dragging an image into a particular location or by highlighting part of an image; in another case, they might indicate which part of a model is incorrect by marking it with an X. It's important to remember that while these tools can be valuable and make many tasks easier or more efficient, they may not be necessary. A task could be constructed to allow students to indicate classification or to identify components of a model without expensive technology, for example.

In this section we explore "Ecosystems," an example of a sophisticated, interactive science program. Our focus is on the ways the designers used the technology to collect information as well as on how you might apply those approaches whether or not you have similar technology.

EXAMPLE 7 **Ecosystems**

Level	**Middle school**
Assesses	**PRACTICES**—Planning and carrying out investigations and interpreting patterns
	CROSSCUTTING CONCEPTS—Systems and system models; Patterns
	DISCIPLINARY CORE IDEAS—Ecosystems: Interactions, energy, and dynamics [LS2]

This is another example that illustrates how technology can enhance an assessment—by making it easy for students to interact with different kinds of material and for the teacher to customize the activities according to her needs. Many of the ideas could be applied even without the technology.

"Ecosystems" is a set of simulation-based modules that middle school students do as part of a curriculum unit on ecosystem dynamics. The modules let students explore representations of particular ecosystems, such as a mountain lake or grassland. The students investigate the roles of different species in a habitat, the relationships among them, and the effects of these interactions on the population levels of each. The instruction is aimed at:

- a *core idea*: the features that are common to all ecosystems;

- a *crosscutting concept*: systems; and

- several *practices*: building and using models, planning and conducting investigations (by manipulating the system elements), and interpreting patterns.

In the course of the unit, the students study what a food web is and how it reflects the flow of matter and energy in the ecosystem. The program includes tasks that can be used for assessment: the students complete them as they get to the appropriate point in their learning. It is difficult to demonstrate all the features of a simulation-based activity in a printed book, but Figure 4-4 gives an idea of how the activity works. It is a screenshot that shows part of a simulated mountain lake environment and the options students would have when it is on their screen. Students observe animations that show how the organisms in this lake (such as algae, shrimp, and trout) interact.

A key feature of the program is that it responds frequently to what the students do. For example, as shown in Figure 4-4, the program prompts the students to draw directly on the screen to represent the way they think the food web would operate in this lake ecosytem. If a student draws an arrow that links a food

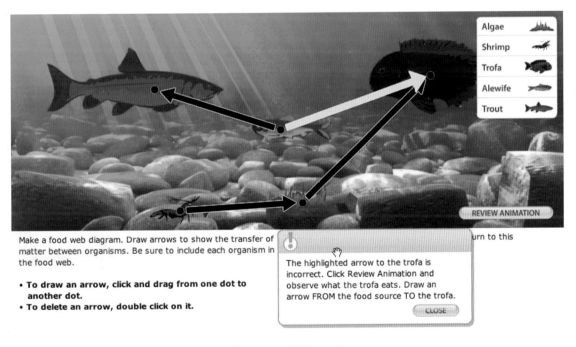

FIGURE 4-4 Screenshot showing simulated mountain lake environment.
SOURCE: Quellmalz et al. (2012, fig. 2, p. 372). Reprinted with permission from John Wiley & Sons, Inc.

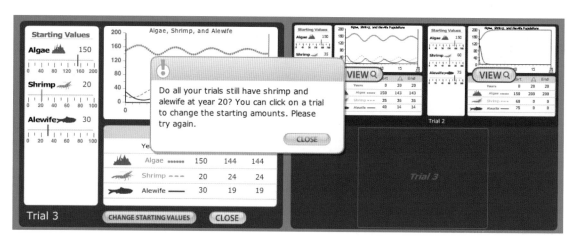

Can you do better than Dr. A? Design three trials so that both the shrimp and alewife populations survive for 20 years.

- **Use the sliders to change the starting numbers of shrimp and alewife.**
- **Click RUN to see what happens.**
- **When you have saved 3 trials in which shrimp and alewife survive for 20 years, click NEXT.**

FIGURE 4-5 Screenshot from ecosystems assessment.

SOURCE: SimScientists Calipers II project (2013). Reprinted with permission.

consumer to the wrong source of matter and energy, a feedback box coaches the student to watch the animation more closely. This is formative feedback that gives students clear direction.

Later in the same module students investigate what happens when the organism populations are varied. As Figure 4-5 shows, the program prompts the students to set different relative population levels for the organisms in the ecosystem at the beginning of a defined time interval. The interactive simulation allows students to conduct multiple trials to see how things change in the ecosystem if there are more shrimp relative to algae levels at the start, for example, or fewer trout compared to alewife.

The students are prompted to draw conclusions about the factors that make an ecosystem healthy and balanced from the data they collect. The program prompts them to develop models of ecosystems and to evaluate how well each represents what the data are showing and the conclusions they have drawn. As students progress through the modules, the program frequently asks them to describe and explain what they have observed and to draw conclusions.

Another key feature of the program is that the teacher can customize these activities to meet her goals. If students are still working to build their understanding, the program can give them immediate feedback. It can also provide a graduated sequence of coaching to help students work through the challenges. Figure 4-6 shows a feedback box for this set of activities, which notifies the student that something doesn't make sense and prompts him or her to correct it. The text at the bottom of the screen lets the student know when to go on to

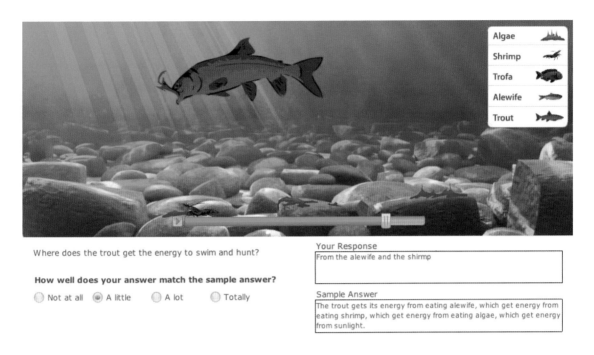

Where does the trout get the energy to swim and hunt?

How well does your answer match the sample answer?

○ Not at all ◉ A little ○ A lot ○ Totally

Your Response

From the alewife and the shirmp

Sample Answer

The trout gets its energy from eating alewife, which get energy from eating shrimp, which get energy from eating algae, which get energy from sunlight.

FIGURE 4-6 Screenshot showing formative feedback.
SOURCE: SimScientists Calipers II project (2013). Reprinted with permission.

the next task, which is analyzing the population graphs and designing three separate trials that will each result in survival for two of the organisms.

Figure 4-6 shows another way the program can provide formative feedback. The student is asked to respond to a question and then is shown a sample answer for comparison. Questions guide the student to think about how he or she might come up with a better response to this sort of question.

When the students are ready, the teacher can set the program to provide less guidance so that she can use the task as a summative assessment. Figures 4-7 and 4-8 show modules from the same program that are used for summative assessment. Students are asked to investigate ways to restore an ecosystem they have not studied—an Australian grassland that has been affected by a significant fire. Neither feedback nor coaching is provided.

Students investigate the animals, birds, insects, and grass by observing animations of their interactions. Based on the interactions they have observed, they draw a food web representing a model of the flow of energy and matter throughout the ecosystem (see Figure 4-7). Next, the program asks them to set up trials similar to the ones done in the formative module about the lake. They can alter the starting populations of crickets and lizards and experiment until they can find three different ratios that will result in both of these species surviving for 20 years. The program also prompts the students to explain their interpretations, draw conclusions, and so forth, but without hints. In a culminating task, students present their findings about the grasslands ecosystem.

Make a food web diagram. Draw arrows to show the transfer of matter between organisms.

Be sure to include each organism in the food web.

- To draw an arrow, click and drag from one dot to another dot.
- To delete an arrow, double click on it.

You can review the animation and then return to this diagram.

FIGURE 4-7 Screenshot showing new ecosystem.

SOURCE: SimScientists Calipers II project (2013). Reprinted with permission.

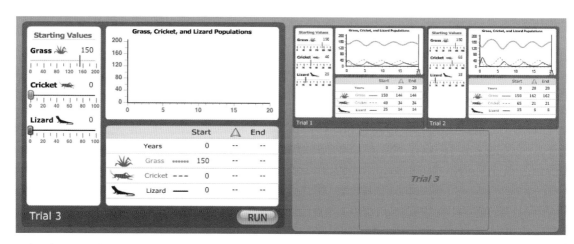

The scientists continue to study the burned grassland. They want to have populations of grass, crickets, and lizards that survive for 20 years.

- **Design three trials to have both the cricket and the lizard populations survive for 20 years.**
- **Use the sliders to change the starting numbers of crickets and lizards.**
- **Click RUN to see what happens.**

When all trials are complete, click NEXT.

FIGURE 4-8 Screenshot from assessment module.

SOURCE: SimScientists Calipers II project (2013). Reprinted with permission.

These assessment modules are designed to address common difficulties students have in reasoning about the components of an ecosystem and the way species behave, as well as their errors in the use of science practices. The simulation generates reports for students about their progress, and teachers can view progress reports for individual students as well as class-level reports. The reports indicate the level of additional aid students may need and can help the teacher group the students to effectively address their areas of difficulty. The program also includes tailored, follow-on reflection activities.

The simulation technology is engaging for students and fun to work with, but those benefits alone might not make it worthwhile. This program engages students in three-dimensional learning through challenging scientific reasoning tasks. Students learn about model-based reasoning in the context of instruction about how ecosystems are structured and how they behave. The task that presents a new ecosystem tests their ability to apply the concepts they learned in studying one ecosystem as they describe the dynamics they observe in a different one they haven't studied.

A commercially available assessment might use simulation without having tasks that measure three-dimensional understanding. Because new software and other technology can be expensive, it's important to be a critical consumer. Some "new" assessments are really the same old types of assessments in a new package, so they might not be worth the added expense. And there may be new applications for devices and programs you already have access to.

You may be able to use certain features of new software to take advantage of the rich context they offer, but you could modify some or all of the tasks, or substitute other activities you devise, to better assess the development of three-dimensional learning over time.

WHAT DO THESE EXAMPLES SHOW US?

"Climate Change" is an example of how a teacher can use an activity for a variety of purposes. The same activity could be used to introduce students to new ideas and practices as well as to guide them in using resources and tools to direct their own learning. It might be adapted to collect information about students' misconceptions so the teacher can respond with instructional interventions right away, or it might be structured as a summative assessment that produces scores that inform parents or others about what students have mastered. "Movement of Water" shows how a fairly simple activity can yield a lot of information if it is designed strategically to provide information a teacher needs at a particular point in instruction. "Ecosystems" is an example of an assessment that uses sophisticated technology to make it easier for a teacher to assess three-dimensional learning that takes place over time. Understanding how this example works can help you as an educator identify assessment technology that is worth a potentially high cost and also see how you might accomplish in other ways some of what the technology makes possible.

CHAPTER HIGHLIGHTS

- Even if your district and state have not adopted new standards that reflect the 2012 framework, or they are not yet revamping their assessments, adapting your own assessments will be a critical aspect of modifying your instruction to engage your students in doing science for themselves and learning in a three-dimensional way.

- The examples in this chapter illustrate more ways to work new assessment ideas into your instruction, adapting activities you already use so they can give you evidence about your students' learning.

- New technology may be an important asset as you make changes, but you can begin by using resources you already have.

5

You and Your School, District, and State

In this chapter we focus on how the changes you make in your instruction can interact with what is happening beyond your classroom and school. We look more closely at how an assessment system can work, how assessment for monitoring purposes can fit with what you do in your classroom, and the importance of the way assessment results are reported. We close with a final example, developed by a teacher, and some ideas about how you can help move your system forward.

WORKING WITHIN AN ASSESSMENT SYSTEM

Most of this book has focused on ideas you can use in your classroom to collect evidence about how your students use science and engineering practices in the context of crosscutting concepts and disciplinary core ideas and how their learning progresses over time. But ideally you are—or soon will be—playing your part in a system of science assessment that is designed around the same vision of science learning.

The most important characteristic of an assessment system is that each of its components is designed with the same set of goals in mind, even if they are used for different purposes. People often distinguish between classroom-based assessments and external assessments, with external ones being those designed or selected by districts or states that are used to monitor learning. This category includes the statewide science tests required for accountability purposes as well as national assessments like the National Assessment of Educational Progress (NAEP) and international ones like the Trends in International Mathematics and Science Study (TIMSS). But this distinction has more to do with the purposes for which the results are used than with the actual design of assessments.

The new frontier in science assessment is to use a variety of assessments that can provide the different sorts of information about student learning that teachers, parents, administrators, the school community, and policy makers need—just as you use a variety of assessment tools in your own classroom depending on what you need the results for.

Components of an Integrated Assessment System

Although this idea is not new, it is nonetheless challenging to implement, and districts and states are just beginning to respond.[1] The challenges of covering the breadth and the depth of the new standards such as the Next Generation Science Standards (NGSS) have made moving to a systems approach even more important. Even a system of assessments won't be able to cover everything included in the curriculum, but a balanced system will include these three components:

1. *Assessments used in the classroom as part of day-to-day instruction.* These may be designed by individual teachers or by developers of curriculum units that include assessment as an integral aspect of the instruction. They may be used for formative or summative purposes, as discussed in Chapter 1.

2. *Assessments designed for monitoring purposes.* Districts and states need to collect information about student learning so that they can monitor the effectiveness of the public education system. Assessments used for this purpose may have many formats and often are like the activities teachers use in instruction. But, to measure the learning of large numbers of students across schools and districts that may have different curricula, states typically use assessments developed outside the classroom so that they are standardized to provide fair and valid measures. They may be administered either at a fixed time or at a time that fits the instructional sequence in the classroom.

3. *Indicators of the quality of instruction and students' access to opportunities to learn and do science.* In a state that is changing its approach to science education, it is especially important to monitor the quality of the instruction students are getting during the transition. These indicators could include, for example, time allocated to science teaching, adoption of instructional materials that reflect the 2012 framework, and classroom coverage of the material in new standards. Districts and states might use program inspections, student

---

[1] A 2006 National Research Council report describes the systems approach to science assessment in detail (National Research Council, 2006).

and teacher surveys, documentation of teachers' professional development, and documentation of classroom assignments of students' work to monitor opportunity to learn.

Assessment for Monitoring

Monitoring student learning on a large scale is an important responsibility for a system, but collecting information about the development of three-dimensional learning on a large scale over time is not easy. Designing assessments for this new challenge involves competing goals. One goal is to rely primarily on performance-based tasks that allow students to actively demonstrate what they can do. Another is to minimize the amount of time students spend on assessments that are needed primarily for external accountability purposes. It is also important to collect information that is reliable enough to support high-stakes decisions, and to do so at an affordable cost.

Practical concerns have made tests used for monitoring and those used in classroom instruction look different. When summative results are needed for large groups of students—as with state assessments—assessment developers are challenged to ensure that the tasks are consistent across the settings in which the students are tested, are affordable, and can cover the material to be tested in a reasonable amount of time.

In the past few decades, experiments with new ways to provide standardized information that can be compared across groups and across time have offered new possibilities for meeting these challenges. One important innovation is that procedures have been developed for using classroom assessments for monitoring purposes. Quality-control procedures can be used to make sure the assessment experience is consistent enough across testing sites and times so that it is fair to compare the results. An example from Queensland, Australia, illustrates how this works.

Queensland has used a system in which exams given to students in grades 11 and 12 are based in their local schools but can be used by the central education authority. The system is set up as a partnership. The central authority establishes the curriculum, but the local schools develop their own programs of study and assessments. Although these have to be approved by the authority, local teachers are nevertheless actively involved in a set of procedures for developing consensus about expectations and performance levels and collecting and scoring student work. Similar procedures are used by the International Baccalaureate program, which bases student grades on a combination of assessments given by teachers and standardized, externally developed tests.

Another strategy that has shown promise is for a central authority, such as a district or state, to use standardized performance assessments that fit naturally into instruction to collect assessment data. For example, a district might ask teachers to spend part of the year on a replacement unit—that is, a curriculum unit designed to provide three-dimensional instruction that includes assessment tasks. This strategy is a way to support teachers in building the new approach into their instruction and can also be a way to collect assessment information.

From an educator's point of view, several aspects of an integrated science assessment system that includes assessments used for monitoring are especially important. The assessments designed for monitoring purposes should be linked closely enough to what you are doing in the classroom so that the results are genuinely useful to you. They should be fair, too, in the sense that students will have had an adequate opportunity to learn so they can perform well on them. This sort of assessment system will also offer many opportunities for teachers to participate in the development and scoring of the assessments. These opportunities are your chance to help make sure that the monitoring assessments actually reflect classroom instruction.

Even though most districts and states offer teachers opportunities to participate in such activities as assessment development, standard-setting, and scoring, teachers have nevertheless had limited influence over most assessments that are developed outside their classrooms. Even if your district or state is not moving quickly toward three-dimensional assessment, you may also play a role in helping your students and their parents interpret assessment results and use the information they provide in a constructive way.

Reporting Results That Work Together

The way assessment results are reported is sometimes taken for granted, but it is critical to making sure that an assessment is used to achieve the beneficial purpose for which it was designed. In an assessment system of the kind we are talking about, the information that is reported, to whom it is provided, and how it is communicated are even more important. A variety of information is collected at different times, using different assessment tools, but the results of each type of assessment coordinate with the results of others.

New assessments will reflect a wide range of science activities and take many forms. Their results will take varied forms too: for instance, they might include graphical displays, descriptive text, reports of numerical scores, and detailed analysis of what the numbers mean. Results might be reported for individual students or for groups, such as all students in a given district or state who are enrolled in fourth grade in a given year. Results might address just one or a few performance expectations or the expectations for an entire year of schooling. A report might place one or a group of students along a numerical scale or just indicate whether the student or students met particular performance criteria. A report might include samples of an individual student's work or anonymous examples of student work that illustrate different levels of performance.

People will be able to use assessment results to take the steps that can improve student learning if those results are presented in a way that is clear and accessible. This means that the reports will need to be designed to meet the needs of different groups—from students, teachers, and parents to state and national policy makers.

Reports will need to include information that explains what was being assessed as well as what sorts of inferences can and cannot be made based on the results. For example, the results of an assessment that asks students to carry out a series of complex tasks—say, designing an investigation, carrying it out, and analyzing and graphing the results—cannot be reported as a single score. Instead, the report should identify the aspects of the set of tasks on which the student or group of students demonstrated competency and where students need further instruction.

As these changes develop, it will be especially important to help parents understand how assessment is evolving and why these changes are important. Your reports to parents are likely to change as you adapt instruction and assessment. Time that you invest in helping your students and their parents learn how they can use new kinds of information will support the changes you are making.

Key Ideas

▶ An integrated science assessment system uses a variety of assessments that can provide the different sorts of information about students' learning that students themselves, teachers, parents, administrators, the school community, and policy makers need. It includes (1) assessments used in the classroom as part of day-to-day instruction, (2) assessments designed for monitoring purposes, and (3) indicators of the quality of instruction and students' access to opportunities to learn and do science.

▶ Clear and accessible reporting of results is as important as the assessments themselves. Reports should explain what was being assessed as well as what sorts of inferences can and cannot be made based on the results. In this way each of the parties who use information about student learning can use it in taking action to improve student learning

HELPING TO SHIFT THE SYSTEM

All of what we've described in this book will take time to implement. Even if your district and state have been among the first to embrace the new approach to science education, the changes will probably occur in stages. There are many ways that you as an individual educator, together with colleagues in your school and district, can participate in and support these changes. We close this chapter with ideas about a few of them.[2]

Addressing Diversity in the Classroom

The student population in the United States grows more diverse every day. Students bring all they have learned from the customs and orientations of their cultural communities to their formal and informal science learning. These are

---

[2]For more ideas, see http://www.nap.edu/catalog/18984 [May 2016].

important resources for classroom instruction. At the same time, it can be challenging to teach in a way that meets the needs of all the students in a class and to assess the learning of students who are not fluent in English or have learning disabilities in a way that is both fair and accurate. A science classroom in which students are actively engaged in doing science is one that presents varied assessment opportunities, but it also intensifies an educator's responsibility to think carefully about ways to value and respect the cultural diversity students bring and how these assets interact with their learning.

Ideas for making sure that instruction engages all students—and is accessible to all—are just as important for new types of assessment.

Build on the Diverse Experiences That Students Bring from Their Homes and Communities

Many aspects of students' everyday lives may offer a pathway to science. Cooking, gardening, tinkering with cars or equipment, spending time in natural settings, doing household chores, tracing family heritage, or traveling to see relatives who live in a different climate are just a few of the activities that can provide oppor-

tunities to ask scientific questions and test hypotheses. You can take advantage of your students' experiences by linking them to what you are teaching and by encouraging them to draw on their skills and experience as they solve problems. Assessments that are a natural part of instruction are opportunities to do the same thing.

Be Aware of Cultural Differences That Can Affect Learning

Experiences that are everyday occurrences for some kids might be unfamiliar to others. Be wary of assuming that all your students will understand a reference or an analogy or will draw the same inferences while doing a task set in a particular context. This does not mean you have to confine classroom discussion to topics and contexts every student already knows well, however. As you get acquainted with the cultural experiences your students bring to the science classroom, you can adjust your instruction and provide additional context and information where it is needed. One way to do this is to allow students to share and discuss their relevant experiences with each other so that they can understand each other's strengths and weaknesses and more effectively work together on projects.

You can also use discussion and other tactics to verify that all students understand the examples or analogies you are using. For example, some students may not have seen the ocean, have had the chance to bake with yeast, or recognize other references that might seem commonplace. Through discussion you can check that the ideas are working as you intended and also see whether your students can suggest experiences and phenomena they've observed that might illustrate a point. This issue is even more important in assessments, where you might get an inaccurate picture of what students understand if the context is unfamiliar to them.

Consider That the Specialized Language of Science Can Be a Particular Challenge for Students Who Are Not Fluent in English

If the testing situation uses scientific terms they haven't yet learned, any students—no matter their fluency in English—will have trouble showing what they know about a particular topic. But a native English speaker may have an advantage in figuring out an unfamiliar term from the context and may have had more opportunities to hear science terms in other contexts than a student who is still learning English. Learning terminology is an important part of science, and helping students understand it is part of good instruction. At the same time, it is important to be sure that an assessment measures only the practices and understanding being targeted. If proficiency in a specialized terminology is not a learning goal in the lesson or unit, then assessment scoring should leave room for students who may, for example, mix up related terminology but still demonstrate understanding of the concepts.

You can use spot assessments to check whether your students are learning terms they need to proceed with a unit—and sometimes you'll want to remind them. The "Climate Change" example in Chapter 4, for instance, illustrates how you might want to give students supports such as definitions while they are working through the stages of a task. Providing a definition at a time when remembering it is not critical to the task is a way to keep exposing your students to the idea. As they encounter and use a term multiple times in different contexts, they can learn it more naturally than if you ask them to memorize it as part of a list. A good assessment will not depend on students' facility with terminology when the goal is to find out what they know about disciplinary core ideas and how well they can use scientific practices.

Provide a Variety of Ways for Students to Demonstrate What They Have Learned, to Reflect the Different Ways Students Learn

Part of making assessments fair is providing multiple ways for students to demonstrate what they know and can do. Assessing something as complex as doing science requires a lot of different kinds of tasks. Giving your students multiple ways to show what they know is also more equitable, and it will give you a more accurate and complete picture of what each of them understands. There will be assessment opportunities in the components of what students are doing: discussing their ideas, collaborating with their classmates, drawing models of what they are thinking, writing out their arguments, designing experiments, and exploring ways to represent data. You can also look for nonverbal ways through which your students can share their ideas: for example, younger students might act out a process or cycle, or they could represent it using clay or small toys. Some older students might create a drawing or a diagram more easily than a written narrative.

Collaborating with Your Colleagues

Perhaps the greatest resource you have is your professional colleagues. Sharing ideas, questions, resources, and experiences with other educators who are adapting their own instruction and assessment practices can have multiple benefits. By joining or helping to establish a professional learning community with this common interest, you can do the following.

Exchange New Ideas and Experiences

Working together may make it easier to adapt activities you are already using. You might start by breaking out elements that you can score or by clustering several activities you are already using so that they work together to give you more information. Exploring comparisons between traditional and new kinds of assessments, such as the one we discussed in Chapter 3, may help you and your colleagues more easily identify assessment opportunities in activities you currently are using. Sharing your ideas and experiences can be an important part of your own reflection on your practice.

Look for other resources that may support your efforts to adapt your assessment practice. For instance, your school may be located near a wetland, a forest, or a body of water. You may live in a region that gets a lot of snow or is in a desert ecosystem. Your community may be wrestling with issues related to pollution, water supply, development, or an invasive or superabundant species. Any of these circumstances might provide an opportunity for activities that that will allow your students to act as scientists: making observations, recording data, analyzing what they have learned, and using what they know about core ideas to develop and test hypotheses. You can use these activities to assess your students' capacity to apply what they've learned in the classroom in a new setting. Your colleagues can also be a source of ideas about and access to these sorts of resources.

Share Information About Performance Expectations for Your Students

As you develop new assessment tasks and rubrics for scoring them, you will need as much information as you can get about how students learn within a particular unit as well as their common misconceptions and stumbling blocks in that unit. Reviewing student work together with your colleagues can help you solidify your understanding and identify examples that reflect levels or stages of performance.

Build Support for and Understanding of the Changes You Hope to Make

Your collaboration with colleagues will help make the changes you are pursuing more visible within your school and district. You and your colleagues can influence priorities and decisions in your school, district, and state by volunteering and speaking up about your efforts and what you are learning. Opportunities to participate in professional activities such as setting standards, scoring, or curriculum development are all chances to learn from others and to share what you have learned in your classroom.

Professional Development and Service Opportunities

This book has emphasized the value of collaborative professional learning communities to help you and your colleagues build new assessment approaches into your instruction.[3] Networks of colleagues provide safe arenas in which to generate ideas, try new things, and compare notes about results. Making these changes will be a process for everyone, and you will want to revise what you are doing as you learn from your experience and your students' responses. Every chance you have to participate in curriculum and assessment design and development teams, assessment scoring sessions, and other collaborative efforts will be an opportunity to learn and to share what you have learned from the exploration you do in your classroom.

School and district leaders can support these changes by providing teachers with opportunities for professional development and collaboration. Teachers who are building the new assessment approach into their practice will be learning, for example, how to:

- use classroom discourse as a means to assess student thinking;

---

[3]For more ideas see http://www.nap.edu/catalog/21836 [May 2016].

- orchestrate classroom discussion to weave together the three dimensions of science learning;

- use specific discussion strategies to support the practice of argumentation;

- identify students' problematic ways of reasoning about disciplinary core ideas and problematic aspects of their participation in practices;

- identify the interests and experiences students bring, so they can build on them throughout instruction;

- understand typical student ideas about a topic and the various problematic alternate conceptions that students are likely to hold; and

- develop models for interpreting students' responses to tasks or questions.

Finding Interdisciplinary Connections

One theme in the new vision for science learning is that students should develop a growing appreciation for the relationships among topics and ideas. A crosscutting concept is one that applies in numerous science disciplines and helps explain many different phenomena. Making these types of connections is important not only within the very broad fields of science and engineering but across other fields as well. Students' abilities to develop reasoned arguments and to marshal evidence and to express their ideas clearly are developed in social studies and English/language arts classes as well as in science classes. They also need to learn how the application of a practice such as argumentation is different in different contexts. Their approaches to thinking about the ethical and social questions raised by many science issues are developed in other classes as well.

The Common Core State Standards and other new standards explicitly call for establishing links across subjects to help students see both how ideas and practices in one area can be applied in another and how study of each enriches them. Because forging these sorts of links is important to the new three-dimensional vision for science education, it is important for science assessment too.

We close *Seeing Students Learn Science* with one last example—this one developed by a teacher. It illustrates a number of the ideas discussed in this book. It engages students directly in doing science and targets interactions between practices and crosscutting concepts and disciplinary core ideas, and it reflects connections across disciplines, among them mathematics, English/language arts, technology, art, and music.

EXAMPLE **8** **SSSNOW Project**

Level   **Grade 6**

Assesses   **PRACTICES**—Planning and carrying out investigations; Analyzing and interpreting data

CROSSCUTTING CONCEPTS—Cause and effect, energy and matter

DISCIPLINARY CORE IDEAS—The role of water in Earth's surface processes [ESS2C]

This example illustrates how a phenomenon in a particular area—in this case, a place that gets a lot of snow during the winter—can be the basis for a unit in which a range of activities are used for instruction and assessment and also to link the science learning to learning in other disciplines—a key goal of the Common Core State Standards.

Students Synthesizing Snow data in Natural Objective Ways (SSSNOW) is an interdisciplinary project developed for sixth graders (Huff and Lange, 2010). Teachers can adapt the basic outlines of this multiple-week project on the physical properties of snow that is designed for schools in snowy climates.

Students begin with some orientation and data collection. Teachers are given access to a variety of online and other resources about weather that they can use to deepen students' understanding of, for example, how moving air masses affect cloud cover. Students can use inexpensive equipment to record outdoor temperatures and snowpack measurements. They conduct more elaborate field investigations as the unit progresses and the snowpack accumulates, digging a snow pit they can use to expose the entire thickness of the snow for study.

Math comes into play as students calculate the density of snow and compare it to that of other materials. They use measures of central tendency both to find ranges in temperatures and to find the mean temperature in a snowpack. Experimentation and research yield information about other properties of snow, including the structure of snow crystals, classification of types of snow, and so on. Students use microscopes to inspect and compare snow samples that vary in age and position in the snowpack.

Students record and analyze their data records. Formative assessments are built into stages of the unit as students discuss their findings and conclusions and use their data to develop explanations for what they have observed. Through videoconferencing technology they share their findings and conclusions and engage in dialogue with National Aeronautics and Space Administration (NASA) scientists. This experience encourages students to consider alternative explanations and refine their thinking.

The connections across disciplines are designed to encourage students to expand their appreciation for what they are observing and how they are thinking about it, for example using nonlinguistic ways to represent what they are learning. Elements such as the ones shown in Table 5-1 are woven together over the course of the unit.

TABLE 5-1 Snow-Related Activities from Different Disciplines

Discipline	Snow-Related Learning Targets/Activities
Science	• Use evidence to support explanations for the causes of phenomena. • Describe properties of matter, including density and hardness. • Identify and describe transfer of energy in a snowpack through the process of conduction. • Identify how the atmosphere, hydrosphere, and lithosphere interact. • Use energy flow to explain changes in systems.
Mathematics	• Make sense of quantities and reason about their meaning. • Construct viable arguments and critique the reasoning of others. • Use technical tools (i.e., thermochrons) to explore and deepen understanding of concepts. • Look for and discern a pattern or structure. • Engage in unit analyses (e.g., centimeters, volume, grams, degrees).
English/Language Arts	• Create murals and read fiction and nonfiction stories of Wilson "Snowflake" Bentley (developer of technique for photographing snowflakes); develop summaries of information. • Construct storyboard panels (illustrations, quotations, summaries, compare/contrast statements) and write reports that explain and argue. • Publish bound books and share with classmates and parents. • Write poetry/haiku. • Create concept maps of snow/winter-related terms.
Technology	• Create and analyze Excel spreadsheet temperature data. • Construct charts, graphs, and concept maps using various apps. • Analyze NASA satellite data for similarities and differences in snowfall rates in Great Lakes region. • Use handheld GPS to determine location.
Art	• Create Japanese kirigami and radial symmetry snowflakes.
Music	• Winter song study and choral presentation.

The teacher who developed this example worked with a colleague to accomplish several different goals with this project. In addition to linking the science activities to objectives in other classes, they also:

- engaged their students in a three-dimensional learning unit that provided the opportunity to collect and analyze data and to draw on many resources as they explored a complex set of questions about water, weather, and energy;

- included formative assessment opportunities that helped them guide their students and also helped the students shape their own research; and

- took advantage of the natural world around their school to get their students outside and learning about phenomena they could observe.

This sort of collaboration will be a critical part of the gradual move to three-dimensional instruction and assessment, and it demonstrates how closely linked these transitions are. Assessment is a fundamental part of instruction. As districts and states adopt new standards, new assessments will be just as important. All the changes associated with adapting to three-dimensional science learning will need to work as a system—and the classroom is at the center of that system. What teachers do every day is essential to students' learning. As you integrate assessment and instruction in your own classroom you will be actively supporting a new, three-dimensional vision of how students learn science.

CHAPTER HIGHLIGHTS

- Adapting the way you weave assessment into instruction in your classroom will contribute to any moves your district and state make toward developing an integrated science assessment system in which useful results are reported to the parties that need them: students, teachers, parents, administrators, and policy makers.

- A science assessment system includes (1) classroom assessments, (2) large-scale assessments used for monitoring, and (3) other indicators of the quality of instruction. It provides accessible results to all who need information about student learning.

- You can contribute to these changes by taking full advantage of cultural differences among your students. Encourage them to share experiences through both verbal (discussions and written assignments) and nonverbal (drawing and diagramming) activities. Factor in non-native English speakers' challenges as you design classroom activities that will be used to assess learning.

- You can also contribute by collaborating with your colleagues: exchanging ideas and feedback, finding interdisciplinary connections, and working together to build support for the changes you hope to make in your classroom and beyond.

References

Farkash, L., Michael, N., Purdie-Dyer, R., McGill, T., Novak, M., and Reiser, B.J. (2016). *Why is our corn changing?: Elementary NGSS 2nd grade unit.* Available: http://www.nextgenstorylines.org/why-is-our-corn-changing [August 2016].

Furtak, E.M., and Heredia, S.C. (2014). Exploring the influence of learning progressions in two teacher communities. *Journal of Research in Science Teaching, 51*(8), 982–1020.

Huff, K., and Duschl, R. (2016). *Get in the Game—Planning and Implementing Coherent Learning Progressions, Sequences, and Storylines.* Unpublished paper.

Huff, K., and Lange, C. (2010). SSSNOW Project: Helping Make Science Cool for Students. *Science Scope, 33*(5), 36–41.

Intergovernmental Panel on Climate Change. (2007). *Climate Change 2007: Impacts, Adaption, Vulnerability.* New York: Cambridge University Press.

Krajcik, J., Reiser, B.J., Sutherland, L.M., and Fortus, D. (2013). *Investigating and Questioning Our World Through Science and Technology.* Second ed. Greenwich, CT: Sangari Active Science.

Lehrer, R. (2011). *Learning to Reason About Variability and Chance by Inventing Measures and Models.* Paper presented at the National Association for Research in Science Teaching, Orlando, FL.

Lucas, D., Broderick, N., Lehrer, R., and Bohanan, R. (2005). Making the grounds of scientific inquiry visible in the classroom. *Science Scope, 29*(3), 39–42.

McGraw-Hill Education. (2008). *Science, A Closer Look, Grade 4, Teacher Edition—Earth Science.* Columbus, OH: Author.

National Research Council. (2000). *How People Learn: Brain, Mind, Experience, and School: Expanded Edition.* Committee on Developments in the Science of Learning. J.D. Bransford, A.L. Brown, and R.R. Cocking, eds. Commission on Behavioral and Social Sciences and Education. Washington, DC: National Academy Press.

National Research Council. (2005). *How Students Learn: Science in the Classroom.* Committee on *How People Learn*, A Targeted Report for Teachers. M.S. Donovan and J.D. Bransford, eds. Division of Behavioral and Social Sciences and Education. Washington, DC: The National Academies Press.

National Research Council. (2006). *Systems for State Science Assessment.* Committee on Test Design for K–12 Science Achievement. M.R. Wilson and M.W. Bertenthal, eds. Board on Testing and Assessment, Center for Education, Division of Behavioral and Social Sciences and Education. Washington, DC: The National Academies Press.

National Research Council. (2012). *A Framework for K–12 Science Education: Practices, Crosscutting Concepts, and Core Ideas.* Committee on a Conceptual Framework for New K–12 Science Education Standards. Board on Science Education, Division of Behavioral and Social Sciences and Education. Washington, DC: The National Academies Press.

National Research Council. (2014). *Developing Assessments for the Next Generation Science Standards.* Committee on Developing Assessments of Science Proficiency in K–12. J.W. Pellegrino, M.R. Wilson, J.A. Koenig, and A.S. Beatty, eds. Board on Testing and Assessment and Board on Science Education, Division of Behavioral and Social Sciences and Education. Washington, DC: The National Academies Press.

National Research Council. (2015). *Guide to Implementing the Next Generation Science Standards.* Committee on Guidance on Implementing the Next Generation Science Standards. Board on Science Education, Division of Behavioral and Social Sciences and Education. Washington, DC: The National Academies Press.

Peters, V., Dewey, T., Kwok, A., Hammond, G.S., and Songer, N.B. (2012). Predicting the impacts of climate change on ecosystems: A high school curricular module. *The Earth Scientist, 28*(3), 33–37.

Quellmalz, E.S., Timms, M.J., Silberglitt, M.D., and Buckley, B.C. (2012). Science assessments for all: Integrating science simulations into balanced state science assessment systems. *Journal of Research in Science Teaching, 49*(3), 363–393.

Reiser, B.J. (2013). Unpublished data from IQWST 6th grade classroom. Collected by Northwestern University Science Practices project. Funded by the National Science Foundation, ESI-1020316 to Northwestern University.

Songer, N.B. et al. (2013). Unpublished resource material from University of Michigan.

Wilson, M. et al. (2013). Unpublished data from the BEAR Center at the University of California, Berkeley.

Resources for Practitioners

Resource	Description	Link
NSTA—NGSS resources	The NSTA offers a variety of resources related to the NGSS as well as forums for discussion and exchange of ideas.	http://ngss.nsta.org
NGSS website—Resources for Teachers	This site provides a compilation of resources designed to help teachers understand the NGSS and design instruction that supports three-dimensional learning.	http://www.nextgenscience.org/teachers
STEM Teaching Tools	This site has tools that can help you teach STEM. They are currently focused on supporting the teaching of the NGSS. Each tool is focused on a specific issue and leverages the best knowledge from research and practice.	http://stemteachingtools.org
The Teaching Channel—videos for science	The Teaching Channel has developed a number of videos related to the NGSS and instruction to support three-dimensional learning.	https://www.teachingchannel.org/videos?page=1&categories=subjects_science&load=1
NGSX—Learning System for Science Educators	NGSX is a Web-based professional development environment designed to engage teachers in working with the practices and disciplinary core ideas in the National Research Council report *A Framework for K–12 Science Education* and the NGSS.	http://www.ngsx.org

continued

Resource	Description	Link
NGSA	The NGSA group is a multi-institutional collaborative that is applying the evidence-centered design approach to create classroom-ready assessments for teachers to use formatively to gain insights into their students' progress on achieving the NGSS performance expectations. They are creating classroom-based, instructionally supportive assessment tasks with accompanying resources that integrate the NGSS dimensions and measure science proficiency. The tasks can be accessed through their task portal.	http://nextgenscienceassessment. org

NOTE: NGSA = Next Generation Science Assessment; NGSS = Next Generation Science Standards; NGSX = Next Generation Science Exemplar System for Professional Development; NSTA = National Science Teachers Association; STEM = science, technology, engineering, and mathematics.

Biographical Sketches of Consulting Experts

Kenneth Huff is a national board certified teacher in early adolescence science with 22 years of classroom experience. Currently, he is a middle school teacher in the Williamsville Central School District in East Amherst, New York. Mr. Huff serves as a member of his district's Staff Development Council, and he founded and leads a Young Astronaut Council for fifth- through eighth-grade students. Mr. Huff also taught at Cleveland Hill Schools in Cheektowaga, New York. In addition to his teaching responsibilities, Mr. Huff is the current president of the Association of Presidential Awardees in Science Teaching, a member of the National Academies of Sciences, Engineering, and Medicine's Teacher Advisory Council, and director at large for professional development for the Science Teachers Association of New York State. Mr. Huff is also a contributing member of the space systems technical committee for the American Institute of Aeronautics and Astronautics. He was a member of the Committee on Middle Level Science Teaching for the National Science Teachers Association (NSTA) and served as chair of the NSTA Aerospace Programs Advisory Board, where he initiated and led the effort to develop a national position statement on aerospace education. A native of New York, Mr. Huff earned his B.S. and M.S. in education from the State University of New York College at Buffalo.

Peter McLaren is the Director of Next Gen Education, LLC. Mr. McLaren was a teacher of science for 13 years at both the high school and middle school levels. He served as science department chair for grades 7–12 for East Greenwich Public Schools in East Greenwich, Rhode Island. Mr. McLaren is currently serving as president of the Council of State Science Supervisors (CSSS), an organization of which he has been a member since 2005. As president of CSSS he also serves on the Alliance of Affiliates of the National Science Teachers Association representing CSSS. Mr. McLaren taught eighth-grade science at Archie Cole Middle School in East Greenwich. In addition to his role as a science teacher, he was also involved as a trainer for several educational technology initiatives such as Project SMART, Rhode Island Teachers and Technology Initiative, and Enhancing Education Through Technology. Mr. McLaren was recognized with the Milken Family Foundation National Educator Award (2001) and as the Rhode Island Science Teacher of the Year (1995) by the Massachusetts Institute of Technology (MIT)-sponsored Network of Educators of Science and Technology. Mr. McLaren is also state coordinator for the Presidential Awards for Excellence in Mathematics and Science Teaching for Rhode Island and has been instrumental in restructuring leadership to reconvene the Rhode Island Science Teachers Association. At the national level, Mr. McLaren has been appointed to a 3-year term as a member of the board of directors for the Triangle Coalition for Science and Technology Education. He is also a member of the Blended Learning Open Source Science or Math Studies Advisory Committee at MIT in Cambridge, Massachusetts. Mr. McLaren has a B.S. in secondary education and an M.A. in science education, both from the University of Rhode Island.

William Penuel is a professor of educational psychology and learning sciences in the School of Education at the University of Colorado Boulder. Professor Penuel began his career in the field of youth development, becoming an expert in program development and evaluation. In his doctoral and early career research, he developed a framework that integrated traditional psychosocial perspectives on identity formation with Vygotskian theories of development. As director of evaluation research at the Center for Technology in Learning at SRI International, Professor Penuel developed a broad program of education research in science, technology, engineering, and mathematics education. Professor Penuel's current research focuses on teacher learning and organizational processes that shape the implementation of educational policies, school curricula, and afterschool programs. He examines learning and development from sociocultural, social capital, and complex social systems perspectives. His teaching interests focus on research methodologies for the learning sciences, adolescent development, and educational technology. Professor Penuel is the author of more than 60 refereed journal articles and conference papers. He serves on the editorial board for *Teachers College Record,* the *American Journal of Evaluation,* and *Cognition and Instruction.* He served as co-chair (with Susan Jurow and Kevin O'Connor) of the 11th International Conference of the Learning Sciences in June 2014. He was previously on the National Research Council's Committee on a Framework for Assessment of Science Proficiency in K–12.

K. Renae Pullen is a current member of the National Academies of Sciences, Engineering, and Medicine's Teacher Advisory Council. She has been an educator in Caddo Parish Public Schools for more than 17 years. Currently, she is the K–6 science curriculum instructional specialist for Caddo Parish. She previously taught both third and fourth grades at Herndon Magnet and Riverside Elementary in Shreveport, and she has been an adjunct professor for Louisiana Technical University (teacher leadership) and Louisiana State University–Shreveport (elementary science methods). Ms. Pullen has received numerous awards and honors, including Walmart Local Teacher of the Year; Caddo Parish Elementary Teacher of the Year; a Fund for Teachers fellowship to study in Spain; a National Endowment for the Humanities fellowship to study the American skyscraper in Chicago, Illinois; numerous grants to support science, technology, engineering, and mathematics (STEM) instruction; and the Presidential Award for Excellence in Science and Mathematics Teaching in 2008. Ms. Pullen has served on several local, state, and national committees and presented at numerous district, state, and national workshops and conferences. In 2011, she participated in the White House Champions of Change Event: Women & Girls in STEM. Ms. Pullen has a B.A. in elementary education from Northwestern State University and an M.Ed. in educational leadership from Louisiana State University in Shreveport, and she is certified as a teacher leader by the State of Louisiana.

Brian Reiser is a professor of learning sciences in the School of Education and Social Policy at Northwestern University. Dr. Reiser was a member of the National Research Council committees that produced the reports *Taking Science to School* (2007), which provided research-based recommendations for improving K–8 science education; *A Framework for K–12 Science Education* (2012), which guided the design of the Next Generation Science Standards (NGSS); and *Developing Assessments for the Next Generation Science Standards* (2014), which provides guidelines for NGSS-based assessments. Dr. Reiser has also worked with Achieve, Inc., to provide feedback on the design of the NGSS and on the tools to help states implement the NGSS, and he is collaborating with several state initiatives to design and provide professional development for K–12 teachers to support them in pursuing the reforms in the NGSS in their classrooms. Dr. Reiser's research examines how to make the scientific practices of argumentation, explanation, and modeling meaningful and effective for classroom teachers and students. Dr. Reiser was a co-leader in the development of IQWST (Investigating and Questioning Our World through Science and Technology), a 3-year middle school curriculum that supports students in science practices to develop core disciplinary ideas. Dr. Reiser received his Ph.D. in cognitive science from Yale University.

Nancy Butler Songer is dean and distinguished university professor in the School of Education at Drexel University. Her research focuses on preparing all American students to become sophisticated thinkers of science and ways to engage and support complex thinkers of science and to improve science learning in high-poverty, urban, elementary and middle school classrooms. Recent recognition includes election as a fellow of the American Association for the Advancement of Science and selection by the U.S. Secretary of Education for the Promising Educational Technology Award. In 1995, she received a National Science Foundation Presidential Faculty Fellowship from President Clinton, the first science educator to receive this recognition. She was previously on the National Research Council's Committee on a Framework for Assessment of Science Proficiency in K–12. Dr. Songer earned an M.S. in developmental biology from Tufts University and a Ph.D. in science education from the University of California, Berkeley.

About the Authors

Alexandra Beatty is a senior program officer with the National Academies of Sciences, Engineering, and Medicine's Board on Testing and Assessment. Since 1996 she has contributed to many projects: among them are an evaluation of the District of Columbia Public Schools; studies of teacher preparation, National Board certification for teachers, and state-level science assessment; and the Committee on Education Excellence and Testing Equity. She has also worked as an independent education writer and researcher. Prior to joining the National Academies staff, she worked on the National Assessment of Educational Progress and College Board programs at the Educational Testing Service. She has a B.A. in philosophy from Williams College and an M.A. in history from Bryn Mawr College.

Heidi Schweingruber is the director of the Board on Science Education (BOSE) at the National Academies of Sciences, Engineering, and Medicine. In this role, she oversees the BOSE portfolio and collaborates with the board to develop new projects. She has worked on multiple National Academies' projects on science, technology, engineering, and mathematics education, including co-directing the study that resulted in the report *A Framework for K–12 Science Education*. She co-authored two award-winning books for practitioners that translate findings of National Academies reports for a broader audience: *Ready, Set, Science!: Putting Research to Work in K–8 Science Classrooms* (2008) and *Surrounded by Science* (2010). Prior to joining the National Academies, she was a senior research associate at the Institute of Education Sciences in the U.S. Department of Education and the director of research for the Rice University School Mathematics Project, an outreach program in K–12 mathematics education. She holds a Ph.D. in psychology (developmental) and anthropology, and a certificate in culture and cognition from the University of Michigan.

Acknowledgments

This book was made possible by the sponsorship of the Carnegie Corporation of New York. It is based on the 2014 National Research Council (NRC) report *Developing Assessments for the Next Generation Science Standards*, which was made possible by the S.D. Bechtel, Jr. Foundation, the Carnegie Corporation of New York, and the William and Flora Hewlett Foundation.

A group of expert practitioners and researchers in the field of science education served as consultants and provided ongoing input in the development of this book. Their invaluable guidance throughout the process is acknowledged with appreciation. This group included Kenneth Huff, Williamsville Central School District, East Amherst, New York; Peter McLaren, Next Gen Education, LLC; William Penuel, School of Education, University of Colorado Boulder; K. Renae Pullen, Caddo Parish Schools, Shreveport, Louisiana; Brian Reiser, School of Education and Social Policy, Northwestern University; and Nancy Butler Songer, School of Education, Drexel University.

Special thanks are also due to Judy Koenig, who helped to ensure that the book was technically accurate and faithful to the parent report on which it is based; and to Kelly Arrington and Matthew Lammers, who provided able administrative support throughout the project. The thoughtful advice contributed by Stephen Mautner of the National Academies Press throughout the process is also gratefully acknowledged.

The final draft of this book was reviewed by individuals chosen for their diverse perspectives and technical expertise. The purpose of this independent review is to provide candid and critical comments that will assist the institution in making the published book as sound as possible and to ensure that the book meets institutional standards for objectivity, evidence, and responsiveness to the charge. The review comments and draft manuscript remain confidential to protect the integrity of the deliberative process.

These six individuals are acknowledged with gratitude for their review of this book: Sarah Bax, Eighth Grade Mathematics Teacher, Hardy Middle School, District of Columbia Public Schools; Catherine Bowler, Administrator for Science and Technology/Engineering Test Development, Department of Elementary and Secondary Education, Malden, Massachusetts; Matthew Krehbiel, Science Associate Director, Achieve, Inc.; Scott Marion, Executive Director, Center for Assessment; Amy L. Reese, Coordinator, Elementary Science, Howard County Public School System, Ellicott City, Maryland; and Darren Wells, Sixth Grade Science and Engineering Teacher, James P. Timilty Middle School, Boston Public Schools.

Although the reviewers listed above provided many constructive comments and suggestions, they did not see the final draft of the book before its release. The review of this book was overseen by Patricia Morison of the National Academies. She was responsible for making certain that an independent examination of this book was carried out in accordance with institutional procedures and that all review comments were carefully considered. Responsibility for the final content of this book rests entirely with the author.

Index

Next Generation Science Standards
    assessment targets, 12
    classroom assessment aligned with, 4
    district and state adoption, 71–73
    learning progressions, 12–13
    performance expectations, 12, 19
    purpose, 5
    three-dimensional framework, 6 n.4, 11, 71
Novak, Michael, 1 n.1

P

Performance expectations
    anchoring instruction in a phenomenon and, 16
    and classroom assessments, 19, 30
    coherence in, 12–13
    examples of students' responses for scoring, 60–61,
        65–67, 68, 69, 78
    learning progressions, 12–14, 24, 29, 65, 66, 67, 68
    scoring rubrics, 58–59, 60–61, 65–66, 69, 100
    targets for assessment, 12, 19, 60–61, 64, 94, 95
    and variation in tasks, 79
Professional development, 11, 23, 25, 29, 92–93, 100–
    101, 109
Purdie-Dyer, Ruth, 1 n.1

Q

Queensland system, 94

R

R+P Collaboratory, 16 n.6
Reiser, Brian, 1 n.1

S

Science literacy, 5
Scientific and engineering practices
    analyzing and interpreting data, 6, 40–46, 47, 48,
        49, 51, 58–65, 68, 69, 73, 74–79, 84–89, 90, 98,
        102–104
    aquatic plants experiment, 7
    arguing from evidence, 6, 33, 34–38, 40, 48, 49, 51,
        58–65, 68, 73, 101, 103
    asking questions, 51, 58–65, 68
    communicating information, 6, 51, 58–65, 68
    constructing explanations, 5, 6, 33, 34–38, 40–46,
        47, 48, 49, 51, 58–65, 68, 73, 79, 80–84, 89–90

    core ideas and crosscutting concepts integrated with,
        6, 9–10, 12
    and development of understanding, 11
    key practices, 6–7
    and learning, 5, 9–10, 12
    mathematics use, 6, 51, 58–65, 68, 102–104
    model development and use, 5, 6, 8, 51, 52-59, 67,
        69, 73, 74-79, 80-90, 98
    planning and carrying out investigations, 6, 40-46,
        47, 48, 49, 51, 58-65, 68, 73, 79, 84-89, 90,
        102-104
Scoring and evaluating work
    and design of assessments, 58, 59, 60–61, 69
    examples of students' responses to tasks used to
        design, 60–61, 65–67, 68, 69, 78
    genetic processes rubric, 65–66, 68
    grouping students into categories and, 68
    informal criteria, 59, 68, 69
    language proficiency and, 98
    learning progressions and, 37–38, 66
    for monitoring assessments, 94
    performance expectations as rubrics, 58–59,
        60–61, 65–66, 69, 100
    red squirrel prediction rubric, 76, 77–78
    silkworm measurement activity, 51, 58–65, 68
    solar system/seasons example, 66–67, 68
    systems approach, 94, 95
    technology and, 79, 83, 84
    validity and reliability, 27
Severance, Sam, 17 n.7
Students Synthesizing Snow data in Natural
    Objective Ways (SSSNOW) Project, 101–104
System approach
    accountability policies, 5, 17, 18, 20, 22, 91,
        93–95
    classroom assessments, 21–22, 23–24, 92, 94,
        96
    collaborating with colleagues, 60, 65, 82, 96,
        99–100, 104
    components of integrated system, 91, 92–93, 94
    diversity considerations in, 26, 92–93, 94
    interdisciplinary connections, 101–104
    International Baccalaureate program, 94
    key ideas, 26, 96
    for monitoring, 22, 23, 24, 27, 28, 30, 31, 71, 91,
        92–95, 96, 105

Photo Credits